FA:

Director:
Fr. Mario Knezović

Editor:
Krešimir Šego

Translator:
Rita Falsetto

Lecturer and Proof Reader:
Rita Falsetto

Croatian Original Title:
Postite srcem

Final Cover Design:
Rita Falsetto

BARBARIĆ, Slavko
      Fast with the heart / Slavko Barbarić ;
(translator Rita Falsetto).
Medjugorje : Informativni centar Mir, 2001
Foreword / Rita Falsetto

ISBN 978-0-9727445-7-7

Fr. Slavko Barbarić

FAST WITH THE HEART

Printed Under Contract by:
The Medjugorje Web
772 N Peace Road
DeKalb, IL 60115
(815)748-0410
http://www.medjugorje.org

INFORMATIVNI CENTAR "MIR" MEĐUGORJE
Međugorje, 2004.

TABLE OF CONTENTS

FOREWORD

Without knowing it, I received an extraordinary gift and a special grace from Our Lady. This grace was to be able to work for and with Father Slavko Barbarić for seven years.

During those years, he quietly guided and taught me by what he lived each and every day in the school of Our Lady - about prayer, about conversion, about fasting.

'Life with bread' was an expression Father Slavko used often in speaking about fasting. That expression has forever been etched in my mind and became a concrete reality for me during these years with him. I came to realize and understand what the word FASTING is meant to stand for: *Forgiveness*, *Acceptance*, *Self-control*, *Truth*, *Integrity*, *Nourishment* and *Grace*.

The purpose of fasting is not to deny ourselves sustenance or to feel hunger, but to grow in the 'inner freedom' necessary to be open to God's graces and love. It compels us, on our emotional, mental, physical and spiritual levels, to reach the purity, humility, peace and joy Our Lady is continually calling us to. I discovered that the goal of fasting is 'perfection and holiness'.

Father Slavko's life was a reflection of a true disciple of Our Lady. She enveloped his very being, and because of this, it was clearly visible that Father Slavko *lived* fasting and prayer. He *lived* conversion. He *lived* the Sacred Scripture. He *lived* the Sacraments. He was a 'living' example of faith, hope, love, forgiveness, peace, joy, patience and humility.

As we know, God is 'perfect love'. I witnessed Father Slavko's immersion in this love through fasting and prayer. He knew that by fasting, one could reach, could feel, and could experience this love—the very essence of 'perfection' in action.

'Fast with the Heart', is the last book written by Father Slavko. It is a key and an answer to the questions of what, why and how concerning fasting in our lives. Through this book, Father Slavko has given a most

9

precious gift to all of us. He left behind a 'signpost' to help us become the 'perfect love' of Jesus Christ.

He begins the book with messages from a dear friend, Our Lady of Medjugorje. He walks us slowly and faithfully through the Old and New Testaments and, like an old confidant, he warmly speaks to us about what the Church, its saints and other religions say about fasting.

He then, with great concern and craft, explains the physical, mental and spiritual aspects of fasting. With gentleness and simple, yet profound, heart filled prayers, he teaches us to speak to Jesus. Finally, he educates us in the nutritional aspects of fasting and includes a few recipes for good measure!

The conclusion by Father Slavko does not end with a 'heavy feeling in one's stomach' about fasting, but is filled with several pages of charmingly witty antidotes pointing to the 'lighter' side of fasting! . . .

. . .and in wisdom, he then finalizes the pages of the book by providing us with a glimpse into what Cardinal Joseph Ratzinger (Prefect of the Congregation for the Doctrine of the Faith in Rome) has said about fasting in our lives as Christians.

As you pray to the Holy Spirit to guide and open your hearts, may you read each chapter of this book with loving expectation so that you can put its contents into practice and become living witnesses of love towards all. In this way, when you are asked by all those God has placed in your life, "How can I, too, reach this perfect love?" From your own experience, may you be able to answer them, "By fasting and prayer."

Through this work of Fr. Slavko and through his intercession, I pray that Our Lady may give you the grace of fasting, prayer and love!

As Father Slavko always wrote, **'Let it be so!'**

Rita Falsetto
Medjugorje, 2001

INTRODUCTION

To speak about fasting at this time of consumerism and its mentality means to speak about a forgotten religious, Biblical and Christian theme. Today not only the practice of fasting, but also its concept are largely lost in the Church. Yet, in the world, more and more is spoken about fasting therapy and various diets that are intended to counteract different illnesses and excess weight. There are an increasing number of clinics that specialize in fasting therapy with very good results, and they attract more and more people who are looking for help. It is known that many modern illnesses are caused by excessive eating and drinking and by a disorderly relationship with food in general. In his peril, man seeks solutions that give him hope. This is why more and more people, individuals and movements, want to return to nature and to a more natural way of life. The sooner more people succeed in returning to a more natural lifestyle, the fewer victims of unnatural living there will be.

Every religion has acknowledged the value of fasting and has requested its followers to fast. Fasting is also known in the revelation of the Old Testament of the Bible. It has always been connected with prayer as a means to peace. Fasting is also accepted in the New Testament. Jesus fasted prior to His public life and said that those who are His own will also fast. The Church tradition knows fasting especially connected with the Eucharist and at times such as Lent and in preparation for feast days. This tradition has been kept for many centuries although recently all traces of fasting have nearly disappeared in the Church. Only Ash Wednesday and Good Friday have remained but even these two days of fasting have lost their real practice and true meaning.

This book originated in the environment of Medjugorje events. The call to fasting surprised many: many consider it to be a matter of exaggeration and fanaticism because we are called to fast on bread and water for two days a week on Wednesdays and Fridays.

Many consider this impossible and, more so, unnecessary. From Our Lady's messages on fasting, however, it is possible to see that She does not think that way. She thinks Biblically and ecclesiastically and She knows that the true and tried conditions for every spiritual growth are fasting and prayer. Reflecting on my own experiences of fasting and the experiences of those who participated in the weekly seminars of fasting and prayer, I can see more and more clearly the unfairness against the practice of fasting in our time, and in this, the unfairness inflicted against proper spiritual growth.

Most respected reader, in this book I entrust to you reflections about fasting and experiences with fasting. I desire to help you understand that fasting is necessary and that it is good to fast both for the body and the soul. Moreover, I desire to help you decide to fast and to experience how good it is to fast.

As I entrust these reflections and experiences to you, I implore God to give you the grace to start fasting and praying so that you may yourself experience that Our Lady is right in calling us to fast and pray.

Medjugorje,
November in the Year of the Great Jubilee

Fr. Slavko Barbarić

I. CALL OF THE QUEEN OF PEACE

According to the witness of the visionaries, Our Lady calls all of us to peace, fasting, prayer and conversion and to a firm faith.

From the beginning of the apparitions until August 14, 1984, fasting was practiced one day a week. On the vigil of the feast of the Assumption in 1984, Ivan the visionary came to the parish office and said that Our Lady appeared to him when he started to get ready for Church. He said that, at this time, Our Lady called everyone to pray all three Mysteries of the Rosary and to fast two days a week, on Wednesdays and Fridays. This call has remained unchanged.

Many were surprised and startled to be called to fast at all, let alone for two days a week. To many, this seemed excessive, unrealistic and impossible. However, even a cursory glance at the history of fasting shows that Jews already fasted two days, on Mondays and Thursdays. The Pharisee in his prayer in the temple thanks God for his prayer, fasting and for giving tithes twice a week. He leaves unjustified because he judged a sinner who prayed in the corner of the temple. (Lk 18,9-13) Jesus did not discard the value of fasting nor did He forbid fasting twice a week. He only forbade judging others.

Mary is the Queen of the Prophets, and all Prophets called for conversion, fasting and prayer as conditions for peace. She does not have any better or different means than those by which the Prophets called to peace, namely, conversion, prayer, fasting and firm faith.

In calling us to fast on two days a week, Mary remains in the tradition of Her Israelite nation and reminds us of the multi-century tradition of the Eastern and the Western Church.[1]

---

[1] Reckinger, Fançois, *Gott begegnen in der Zeit: unser Kirchenjahr*, Verlag bonifatius Drickerei, Paderborn, 1986., p. 73.

While the Second Vatican Council calls everyone to return to 'the source', we must admit that we have not discovered fasting but, instead, the opposite has happened. In the past decades, fasting has been reduced to the least possible measure – to two days a year: Ash Wednesday and Good Friday.

The apparitions in Medjugorje have not presented anything new nor have they revealed anything unknown. Instead, they help us accept what God asked for through the prophets – what Mary did and Jesus Himself has done.

In several of Her messages, Mary has spoken about fasting.

August 14, 1984

This apparition was unexpected. Ivan was praying at home and then started to get ready to go to Church for the evening services. By surprise Our Lady appeared to him and told him to relate this message to the people:

"I would like the people to pray along with me these days. And to pray as much as possible! And to fast strictly on Wednesdays and Fridays, and every day to pray at least one Rosary: the Joyful, Sorrowful and Glorious Mysteries."

Our Lady asked that we accept this message with a firm will. She especially requested this of the parishioners and the faithful of the surrounding area.

September 20, 1984

"Dear children!
Today I call on you to begin fasting with the heart. There are many people who are fasting, but only because everyone else is fasting. It has become a custom, which no one wants to stop. I ask the parish to fast out of gratitude because God has allowed me to stay this long in this parish. Dear children, fast and pray

with the heart. Thank you for having responded to my call."

Mary calls us to pray with the heart and to fast with the heart. This means to pray and fast with love; and love for God and others is the sole and true motivation for prayer and fasting. In a Biblical sense, no other motivation is sufficient.

September 26, 1985

"Dear children!

I thank you for all the prayers. Thank you for all the sacrifices. I wish to tell you, dear children, to renew the messages, which I am giving you. Especially live the fast, because by fasting you will achieve and cause me the joy of the whole plan, which God is planning here in Medjugorje, being fulfilled. Thank you for having responded to my call."

Prayer and fasting are a way to joy but also a condition for the realization of what God has planned here in Medjugorje. Without prayer and fasting, God's plans cannot be realized. Our cooperation is very important. So many times Our Lady has repeated that She needs us in the realization of the plans God has entrusted to Her.

September 4, 1986

"Dear children!

Today again I am calling you to prayer and fasting. You know, dear children, that with your help I am able to accomplish everything and force Satan not to be seducing to evil and to remove himself from this place. Dear children, Satan is lurking for each individual. Especially in everyday affairs he wants to spread confusion among each one of you. Therefore, dear children, my call to you is that your day would be only prayer and complete surrender to God. Thank you for having responded to my call."

Fasting and prayer are the best means in the battle against Satan. Only by prayer and fasting can Satan be forced to withdraw from his evil plans and be distanced from the faithful in general and from this place. Jesus said to the disciples that there are kinds of evil spirits which cannot be cast out except by prayer and fasting. (Mk 9, 29)

December 4, 1986

"Dear children!

Today I call you to prepare your hearts for these days when the Lord particularly desires to purify you from all the sins of your past. You, dear children, are not able by yourselves, therefore I am here to help you. You pray, dear children! Only that way shall you be able to recognize all the evil that is in you and surrender it to the Lord so the Lord may completely purify your hearts. Therefore, dear children, pray without ceasing and prepare your hearts in penance and fasting. Thank you for having responded to my call."

Fasting and prayer are a means through which we open ourselves to God, Who can cleanse us of all the sins of our past. Alone we cannot help ourselves and without prayer and fasting, we cannot recognize the evil that wants to destroy us. Preparation of hearts for cooperation with God takes place in prayer and fasting.

July 25, 1991

"Dear children!

Today I invite you to pray for peace. At this time peace is being threatened in a special way, and I am seeking from you to renew fasting and prayer in your families. Dear children, I desire you to grasp the seriousness of the situation and that much of what will happen depends on your prayers and you are praying a little bit. Dear children, I am with you and I am inviting you to begin to pray and fast seriously as in the first days of my coming. Thank you for having responded to my call."

16

Prayer and fasting are a means of protecting the endangered peace. Mary not only calls individuals but also families to pray and to fast so that evil may be stopped. This call is serious because what will happen in the world depends on how much we pray and fast. We recall how the prophet Jonah called the Ninevites to prayer and fasting so that the city would not be destroyed. Everyone fasted and prayed and the city was spared.

August 25, 1991

"Dear children!

Today also I invite you to prayer, now as never before when my plan has begun to be realized. Satan is strong and wants to sweep away plans of peace and joy and make you think that my Son is not strong in his decisions. Therefore, I call all of you, dear children to pray and fast still more firmly. I invite you to renunciation for 9 days so that with your help everything I desired to be realized through the secrets I began in Fatima may be fulfilled. I call you, dear children, to grasp the importance of my coming and the seriousness of the situation. I want to save all souls and present them to God. Therefore, let us pray that everything I have begun be fully realized. Thank you for having responded to my call."

When Satan threatens God's plans, then the Queen of Prophets, as all prophets would, calls to more ardent fasting and prayer. This is so that Satan can be confounded in his plans of destruction and ruin in God's plans, which were especially revealed in the Fatima messages. It is actually a matter of salvation and of realization of everything God has entrusted to Mary, the Queen of Peace and the Queen of Prophets.

March 25, 1992

"Dear children!

Today as never before I invite you to live my messages and to put them into practice in your life. I have come to you to help you and, therefore, I invite you to change your life because you have taken a path of misery, a path of ruin. When I told you: convert, pray, fast, be reconciled, you took these messages superficially. You started to live them and then you stopped, because it was difficult for you. No, dear children, when something is good, you have to persevere in the good and not think: God does not see me, He is not listening, He is not helping. And so you have gone away from God and from me because of your miserable interest. I wanted to create of you an oasis of peace, love and goodness. God wanted you, with your love and with His help, to do miracles and, thus, give an example. Therefore, here is what I say to you: Satan is playing with you and with your souls and I cannot help you because you are far away from my heart. Therefore, pray, live my messages and then you will see the miracles of God's love in your everyday life. Thank you for having responded to my call."

We have taken the messages of fasting and prayer superficially and without seriousness. That is why Mary is saying that Satan is playing with our souls. He is the enemy who can be conquered only by fasting and prayer. Mary is sad that we turned away from Her messages and that we do not live them. She desires to create 'an oasis of peace' of us but what will happen depends on us.

April 25, 1992

"Dear children!

Today also I invite you to prayer. Only by prayer and fasting can war be stopped. Therefore, my dear little children, pray and by your life give witness that you are mine and that you belong to me, because Satan wishes in these turbulent days to seduce as many souls as possible. Therefore, I invite you to decide for God and He will protect you and show you what you should do and which path to take. I invite all those who have said "yes" to me to renew their consecration to my Son Jesus and to His Heart and to me so we can take you more intensely as instruments of peace in this unpeaceful world. Medjugorje is a sign to all of you and a call to pray and live the days of grace that God is giving you. Therefore, dear children, accept the call to prayer with seriousness. I am with you and your suffering is also mine. Thank you for having responded to my call."

Even wars can be stopped by prayer and fasting. This is one of the first messages Our Lady gave. Fasting and prayer can stop even natural disasters. Peace also depends on prayer and fasting. We need to understand this with seriousness. Mary is with us and suffers with us.

November 25, 1996

"Dear children!

Today, again, I invite you to pray, so that through prayer, fasting and small sacrifices you may prepare yourselves for the coming of Jesus. May this time, little children, be a time of grace for you. Use every moment and do good, for only in this way will you feel the birth of Jesus in your hearts. If with your life you give an example and become a sign of God's love, joy will prevail in the hearts of men. Thank you for having responded to my call."

Our Lady gave us this message just at the beginning of the Christmas season. Prayer and fasting are a means by which we can prepare ourselves for the coming of Jesus. Only by prayer and fasting can our hearts be cleansed and completely opened to His coming. Prayer and fasting free man from incorrect relationships with himself, with God, with others and especially with material things.

March 25, 1998

"Dear children!

Also today I call you to fasting and renunciation. Little children, renounce that which hinders you from being closer to Jesus. In a special way I call you: Pray, because only through prayer will you be able to overcome your will and discover the will of God even in the smallest things. By your daily life, little children, you will become an example and witness that you live for Jesus or against Him and His will. Little children, I desire that you become apostles of love. By loving, little children, it will be recognized that you are mine. Thank you for having responded to my call."

Prayer and fasting help us to turn away from everything that hinders us from coming closer to Jesus. We must conquer our own will and open ourselves to the will of God. In this way, we become witnesses for Jesus and apostles of His Love; we become recognizable signs of God's presence in the world. By prayer and fasting, we must achieve inner freedom from everything that separates us from Jesus.

October 25, 1998

"Dear children!

Today I call you to come closer to my Immaculate Heart. I call you to renew in your families the fervor of the first days when I called you to fasting, prayer and conversion. Little children, you accepted my messages with open hearts, although you did not know what prayer was. Today, I call you to open yourselves completely to me so that I may transform you and lead you to the heart of my son Jesus, so that He can fill you with His love. Only in this way, little children, will you find true peace -- the peace that only God gives you. Thank you for having responded to my call."

At the beginning of the apparitions many people fasted and prayed. Over time, forgetfulness and fatigue set in. Mary calls us to again return to the initial fervor and to accept prayer and fasting so that our hearts may be completely open and that our transformation can continue. We are called to become similar to the Heart of Jesus and to Mary's Heart. Prayer and fasting are conditions for opening ourselves to the peace God gives.

II. EXPERIENCE OF FASTING

2.1. A Witness of a Priest

Along with pilgrims, many priests have come to Medjugorje. There they have discovered personal prayer, joy in Confession, joy in the celebration of Holy Mass and the meaning of their priesthood in general. I gladly recall an experience of a pilgrim priest who admitted that he discovered fasting in Medjugorje.

He wrote about his experience:

"I have been a priest for 30 years. There are very few Sundays that I have not celebrated Holy Mass with the faithful. Even when I went on vacation, I had often to return to my parish on Sunday to celebrate Holy Mass with them because I could not find a replacement. I am certain that during my entire priesthood I celebrated Holy Mass with them and preached to them every Sunday of Lent without exception.

In Medjugorje, I became aware that I had completely forgotten about fasting. I never preached about fasting. I did not try to inspire the faithful to fast nor had I explained why it was necessary to fast. If I said anything about fasting, it was that good works could substitute for it. I had also completely lost sight of the Eucharistic fast.

Now that I have discovered fasting, I am surprised at how it was possible for me not to have recognized this Biblical practice and message and not to have proclaimed it to the people. When I read the Sacred Scripture now, I find many places where fasting is spoken about and how the prophets and their nation practiced it. I now recognize the fact that Jesus Himself fasted.

When I started to fast, I discovered the value of fasting and I now often speak to the people about how important it is to fast and pray.

I believe that something similar has happened to other priests. Enriched by this new experience, I would like to call all priests and preachers to compensate for this neglect, which should not have happened at all, in their preaching and in their personal practice."

2.2. The Witness of a Religious Sister

Many faithful responded to Mary's call to fasting. In conversational format, a sister who desires to remain anonymous witnesses:

What did you experience when you heard Our Lady's call to fasting?

I know that I felt a great joy even though I did not understand why I was particularly joyful about this message of fasting. Now, after much experience of fasting and more than 18 years since the beginning of Our Lady's call, it seems to me that I was joyful about fasting because I felt that I was also able to do 'something'. I sensed a change because fasting had really been forgotten.

Did your family fast?

Yes. I especially remember how hard we worked, but still ate only bread and onions. That was always something exceptional. We fasted every Friday - and not only during Lent. On Ash Wednesday and on Good Friday, we did not eat fish in our family as some others did. To eat fish was a real feast in our family so we only ate bread on those days. Also, it was important to me that during Lent, no songs other than Lenten songs could be sung. Radio and television would only be turned on for the news.

Afterwards when I grew up, it was said that fasting could be replaced with something else. Some said that they would not drink or smoke during Lent or that they were renouncing sweets - and fasting disappeared. I remember that we spoke about fasting. I will never forget when I first found out that Muslims fast strictly for a period of time. I was always somehow sad that we

Christians did not fast more. This is why the call to fasting was like a new light for me. I was convinced that something new would also take place in our Church as a result of this call.

Do you remember something particular about the time when you started to fast in response to Mary's call?

I now recognize two phases in my fasting. The first phase was one of fasting only because Our Lady called us to fast. Those were always days of joy. I baked bread, ate it and rejoiced. It was so sweet, tasty and beautiful. It did not dawn on anyone to complain and we all realized that it was possible. No one spoke about any danger of fasting or had any doubt about being able fast.

I had a special experience at work. Some people who worked with me were from Medjugorje and every day I asked them about what Our Lady said. The day they told me that Our Lady asked for fasting on Fridays on bread and water, I was the first to come to our cafeteria to take bread and water. When others asked me, "Is there nothing else for lunch?" I responded, "Whoever sits at my table should take bread and water because Our Lady is calling us to fast in this way." Many only took bread and water. Nearly everyone fasted and no one was upset not even the cooks. From that day on, I fast on Wednesdays and Fridays with bread and water as Our Lady has asked. On other days, I take fruit.

I experienced a similar delight when I understood that we are called to read the Sacred Scripture every day. From the Altar, the parish priest asked us to promise then and there to do this. True delight overcame me. I decided to begin reading the Sacred Scripture. It was the daily reading of It that started to change my life. Before I heard that we should read Sacred Scripture, but I never started to. Somehow, it always seemed distant to me. Now I am able to say that by reading the Word of God every day, I fell in love with Jesus Christ. In Him, I found what I searched for with all my soul.

What happened in the second phase of your fasting?

I read in a book that the meaning of fasting 'a life with bread' is to bring us closer to the Eucharist, because Jesus remains with us in 'the Bread'. It is then that I discovered a deep meaning of fasting for myself and this delighted me. Up to then, I fasted out of love and obedience towards Our Lady. I wanted to fulfill Her desire. But over time, a deep longing to live with the 'bread' and to be closer to Jesus came about. That desire has never left me and I continually want to be closer to Jesus in the Eucharist. In this way, my relationship with the Holy Mass and Adoration changed.

So, you discovered a connection between prayer, Adoration and fasting?

I can really say that it is not possible to fast if there is no time for prayer. Adoration is especially important to me (to be close to Jesus) regardless of how I spend that time - whether I am concentrating, distracted, tired or rested. It is important for me to be close to Jesus. Even though I experienced that it was much easier to fast when I prayed and adored Jesus, there were also days that were very difficult. There were days of trials and of a strange burden upon me, when all that carried me through the fast day, would vanish. On such days, I exerted all my strength and I perseveringly continued. It was on the beautiful days which were full of joy, peace and inner strength that I understood that it is God's will for me to fast. The beautiful and difficult days would interchange.

Did you start to fast more than just on Wednesdays and Fridays?

This is true. In the meantime, I went to the convent and decided for a religious vocation. It is then that novenas started to delight me. I am not sure how or why but I started preparing myself for feast days with prayer and fasting. During these novenas I did not only fast on bread, but also I reduced all food intake to a minimum. During the war, I naturally fasted for more novenas in addition to those for feast days. Each month I did at least one novena. Sometimes I would take a calendar and look for feast days. In a year, there are as many novenas as there are months and a few more. If some of the feast days were close to each other, I would do a novena in addition to a three-day preparation. In this way, I wanted to help with my contribution. When I came to serve in Medjugorje, I started to fast more strictly. During Advent and Lent, I started to fast every day except on Sundays and experienced that this was possible. This Jubilee year, I desire to become closer to the most Holy Trinity and I am trying to fast more.

Have you had special experiences with novenas?

Every novena is a special experience for me. However, after stricter novenas on bread and water, I experienced an indescribable nearness of God on the actual feast day. This gave me strength and lasted for nearly two years. This grace was a gift for the fast days.

I will not forget a grace I received one year for the feast of Christ the King. I prepared myself by fasting strictly. During communion, I felt God's complete nearness, followed by a closeness to all people as brothers and sisters. I felt a great love for everyone in the Church and for all the people in the world. When God's nearness became more and more intense I said, "No, my God. I want you to give this grace to all people first and only then to give it to me." By this, I consciously renounced all the graces received during my novenas. I knew what I was saying. Such experiences then stopped. Sometimes I was sad because of this, but I was always joyful because I knew what I was doing and that was fine.

You spoke about the change of your relationship with others?

Much has changed. It is impossible to put into words or to express. I would like to convey the joy and experience of God to everyone regardless of what others may think of me. Whenever I speak I feel at risk but I am not afraid. In the experience of love for others, I actually first felt my own weaknesses. Everything came to the light. When I saw a weakness in myself that I criticized in someone else, it was easier for me to forgive them and to continue loving them. This is why I cannot judge others and I understand their weaknesses. All these are graces I received through fasting.

At this time, communities do not fast. How has your community accepted your fasting?

At the beginning there were difficulties and there was opposition because of a fear that something would happen to me because of fasting - that I would get sick. But I had the strength to remain on my path and to remain faithful to Our Lady. I was convinced that this was God's will and that Our Lady would not ask for something impossible. However, one needs to be prudent. Enough liquids must be taken. My own experience confirms that when I fast I am protected in a special way and that it is not dangerous at all to fast. During fasting, a lightness of the body takes place and I can pray and work more. I can endure more. During the days of fasting, I overcome everything by my surrender to God. For me, a day of fasting is always a day of prayer and Adoration and somehow this has become my life. When I do not fast, I feel the weight of my body and that I cannot go further – I become tired.

You discovered bread, but did you also have an experience with water?

For a long time, I really concentrated on bread and I came to understand more profoundly 'why bread'. On the feast of the Baptism of the Lord, a reflection concerning water also awakened in me. I felt a deep desire to truly be Christian and to enter into the depths of Christianity by looking at how the early Christians lived. They were strong in their faith and endured everything because they looked to Christ. I started to learn from them. Whenever I drank water while fasting, I received a gift of seeing the baptism of Our Lord and the blessed water He was baptized by. Every time I drank water, a prayer from the Psalm came to me "Wash me of my iniquity O Lord, and cleanse me from my sin." My experience with bread also deepened. Whenever breaking the bread, these words come to my heart, "My God is the Bread that is broken and given to all." In this way, fast days become a ceaseless prayer.

I will never forget when I first realized the extraordinariness of the drop of water being poured into the chalice by the priest and intermingling with the wine. This drop of water is a challenge and a call for me to become small and pure like it. Since then, the yearning within me to be cleansed and purified has grown even stronger as my heart repeats, "Wash me, cleanse me, anoint me . . ."

What else would you like to recommend to the religious brothers and sisters?

Simply that we be 'Christian' and be recognized as such. Like everyone else, we all need to be cleansed and purified from cursing, drugs, conflicts, arguments and interpersonal judgments. We cannot be recognized as Christian when we behave like that. It is my desire that we bring fasting back into our lives and that we may experience God. This is possible. God continually wants to purify us so that we can live like real Christians. Those of us who are consecrated must be a sign of love and peace among other consecrated people so that, in this way, we can serve them even better for the glory of God. Let us fast and pray not to fall into the temptation of living only for ourselves, but that we may live for others. I promise everyone to include them in my fasting and prayer. I hope that the Lord will make us capable of witnessing His Eucharistic love and spreading His peace.

III. FASTING AND ITS FRUITS IN THE PRAYERS OF THE CHURCH

There is an old rule in the Church: 'the law of prayer – the law of faith' *(lex orandi – lex credendi.)* This meant: what was believed and done was expressed in prayer; then the faithful prayed again and what was expressed in prayer was actually realized in life. When we look at the prayers and hymns of the Church during Lent, it is very evident what the Church has done, prayed and believed. Even at first glance, such prayers reveal what fasting meant and what it should mean for Christians.[2]

"Lord, protect us in our struggle against evil. As we begin the discipline of Lent, make this day holy by our self-denial." (Ash Wednesday, opening prayer) *

* The Croatian Roman Missal reads "Lord, we start this lent of fasting, prayer and brotherly love. Grant us strength against the attacks of evil and perseverance in good works."

Fasting, prayer and good works are a means through which we are strengthened against the spirit of evil and by which we persevere in good works.

Fasting is a means that gives us strength to change our lives and to discover God's love and mercy. That is why in the antiphon to the blessing of the ashes on Ash Wednesday we pray:

"Come back to the Lord with all your heart; leave the past in ashes, and turn to God with tears and fasting, for He is slow to anger and ready to forgive."

In the prayers of the Ash Wednesday Mass, fasting is understood as a remedy against evil desire and a cleansing from sin - as medicinal for us and pleasing to God.

---

[2] *The Roman Missal*, Catholic Book Publishing Co., New York 1985., pp. 76-121.

"Lord, help us to resist temptation by our Lenten works of charity and penance. By this sacrifice may be prepared to celebrate the death and resurrection of Christ our Savior and be cleansed from sin and renewed in spirit." (Ash Wednesday, prayer over the Gifts)

" . . .Lord, through this communion may our Lenten penance give you glory and bring us your protection." (Ash Wednesday, prayer after Communion) *

* The Croatian Roman Missal reads, "May our fasting be pleasing to you and healing to us."

"Father, you increase our faith and hope, you deepen our love in this communion. Help us to live by your words and to seek Christ, our bread of life, who is Lord for ever and ever." (First Sunday of Lent, prayer after Communion) *

* The Croatian Roman Missal reads, "Lord, you filled us with the bread from heaven through which faith is nurtured, hope renewed and love strengthened. We ask you to teach us to hunger for Jesus Christ, the living and real bread and to live from every word that comes from your lips."

This means that the life with bread, to which Our Lady calls us, helps us to live from every word that comes from God's lips. Fasting means discipline for the body and a freeing of the soul so that it can yearn for God.

"Father, look on us, your children. Through the discipline of Lent help us to grow in our desire for you." (Tuesday, First Week of Lent, opening prayer) *

* The Croatian Roman Missal reads, "Look upon your family Lord: in renunciation, our body finds beneficial discipline. Grant that our soul may burn with desire for you."

The Church further prays for the corporeal renunciation to give birth to spiritual fruits. In this, it shows the connections between fasting and spiritual fruits.

"Lord, may this sacrifice bless our Lenten observance. May it lead us to sincere repentance." (Thursday, Second Week of Lent, prayer over the gifts) *

* The Croatian Roman Missal reads, "Lord, sanctify our fasting by this sacrifice. Help true conversion of the heart correspond to the external Lenten penance."

This prayer touches on a great problem. Because of it, Jesus often disputed with the Pharisees. He attacked their fasting and prayer because it was done for the sole reason of being praised by others, without an effort of harmonizing their interior life with their actions. The one who prays and fasts must pray for the grace of fasting and prayer. He must pray for the interior journey of his heart to accord with his external actions. If this does not take place, then both fasting and prayer come into question. Prayer and fasting must prepare a person's heart for the Easter celebration. This is their primary meaning.

The Church also recognizes God's concern for us sinners when It prays:

"Father, you have taught us to overcome our sins by prayer, fasting and works of mercy. When we are discouraged by our weakness, give us confidence in your love." (Third Sunday of Lent, opening prayer) *

* The Croatian Roman Missal reads, "God, you who are the source of mercy and all goodness, you have decreed a remedy for our sins: fasting, prayer and acts of love. We admit that we are sinful. Our conscience accuses us. We ask You to always render Your mercy to us."

Fasting, just like renunciation, gives strength, enables us to pray and brings joy.

"Lord, during this Lenten season nourish us with your word of life and make us one in love and prayer." (Wednesday, Third Week of Lent, opening prayer) *

* The Croatian Roman Missal reads, "Lord, grant that by this Lenten renunciation and by listening to your word we may be strengthened in our faithfulness to you and be united as one in prayer."

"Lord, may this Lenten observance of the suffering, death and resurrection of Christ bring us to the full joy of Easter." (Saturday, Third Week of Lent, opening prayer)

Lenten devotion, namely, fasting, prayer and acts of love enable a person to be a witness and a messenger of salvation to the world. They enable him to experience conversion, to be fortified in good works and to be healed.

"Lord, may our Lenten observance prepare us to embrace the paschal mystery and to proclaim your salvation with joyful praise." (Tuesday, Fourth Week of Lent, opening prayer)

"Merciful Father, may the penance of our Lenten observance make us your obedient people. May the love within us be seen in what we do and lead us to the joy of Easter." (Thursday, Fourth Week of Lent, opening prayer) *

* The Croatian Roman Missal reads, "Lord we humbly pray to you: convert our hearts with penance and fortify us in good works to fulfil your commandments and soundly arrive to Easter joy."

In the preface of Lent, the Church sings about the role of Jesus' fasting, which also must be the same for us, Christians.

"His fast of forty days makes this a holy season of self-denial. By rejecting the devil's temptations he has taught us to rid ourselves of the hidden corruption of evil, and so to share his paschal meal in purity of heart, until we come to its fulfillment in the promised land of heaven." (Preface, First Sunday of Lent)

"Each year you give us this joyful season when we prepare to celebrate the paschal mystery with mind and heart renewed. You give us a spirit of loving reverence for you, our Father, and of willing service to our neighbor. As we recall the great events that gave us new life in Christ, you bring the image of your Son to perfection within us." (Preface, First Sunday of Lent) *

* The Croatian Roman Missal reads, "Each year you grant for us to jubilantly wait for the Easter joy, to purify our souls by penance and to eagerly pray and carry out acts of love."

"This great season of grace is your gift to your family to renew us in spirit. You give us strength to purify our hearts, to control our desires, and so to serve you in freedom. You teach us how to live in this passing world

with our heart set on the world that will never end."
(Preface, Second Sunday of Lent)

"You ask us to express our thanks by self-denial. We are to master our sinfulness and conquer our pride. We are to show to those in need your goodness to ourselves."
(Preface, Third Sunday of Lent)

"Through our observance of Lent you correct our faults and raise our minds to you, you help us grow in holiness, and offer us the reward of everlasting life through Jesus Christ our Lord." (Preface, Fourth Sunday of Lent)

What the Church has prayed, believed and what It has called the faithful to do is clearly visible from the above-noted prayers. It is not difficult to see the discrepancy between what is proclaimed and said about fasting today, and what is approved by the Church.

IV. FASTING IN THE BIBLE

In Biblical revelation, fasting is connected with the call to prayer and conversion. Prophets fasted before accepting their service as prophets and before special revelations. Individuals fasted in various circumstances of life - of joy, gratitude, sorrow, and sinfulness. Even the entire nation fasted in preparation for certain feasts; to be saved from a catastrophe; or to come out of a catastrophe once they had fallen into it.

Texts and situations pertaining to fasting, as set out in the Old and in the New Testament, follow according to their themes:

THE OLD TESTAMENT

4.1. Fasting and Visions

Then the Lord said to Moses, "Write down these words for in accordance with them I have made a covenant with you and with Israel. So Moses stayed there with the Lord for forty days and forty nights, without eating any food or drinking any water, and he wrote on the tablets the words of the covenant, the Ten commandments." (Ex 35,27-28)

"When I had gone up to the mountain to receive the stone tablets of the covenant, which the Lord made with you. Meanwhile I stayed on the mountain forty days and forty nights without eating and drinking till the Lord gave me the two tablets of stone inscribed by God's own finger with a copy of all the words that the Lord spoke to you on the mountain from the midst of the fire on the day of the assembly. Then, at the end of the forty days and forty nights, when the Lord had given me the two stone tablets of the covenant." (Dt 9,9-11)

"In the third year of Cyrus, king of Persia, a revelation was given to Daniel, who had been named Belteshazzar. The revelation was certain: a great war; he understood it from the vision. In those days, I, Daniel, mourned

three full weeks. I ate no savory food, I took no meat or wine, and I did not anoint myself at all until the end of the three weeks.

On the twenty-fourth day of the first month, I was on the bank of the great river, the Tigris. As I looked up, I saw a man dressed in linen with a belt of fine gold around his waist. His body was like chrysolite, his face shone like lightning, his eyes were like fiery torches, his arms and feet looked like burnished bronze, and his voice sounded like the roar of a multitude. I alone, Daniel saw the vision: but great fear seized the men who were with me; they fled and hid themselves, although they did not see the vision. So, I was left alone, seeing this great vision. No strength remained in me; I turned the color of death and was powerless." (Dn 10,1-8)

4.2. Lamentation of Sins

The Israelites forgot their true God and followed false gods. Samuel said:

Samuel said to them: "If you wish with your whole heart to return to the Lord, put away your foreign gods and your Ashtaroth, devote yourselves to the Lord, and worship Him alone. Then he will deliver you from the power of the Philistines. So the Israelites put away their Baals and Ashtaroth, and worshiped the Lord alone. Samuel then gave orders, 'Gather all Israel to Mizpah, that I may pray to the Lord for you.' When they were gathered at Mizpah, they drew water and poured it out on the ground before the Lord and they fasted that day, confessing, 'We have sinned against the Lord.' " (1 Sm 7,3-6)

"Have you found me out, my enemy?" Ahab said to Elijah. 'Yes,' he answered. 'Because you have given yourself up to doing evil in the Lord's sight, I am bringing evil upon you: I will destroy you and will cut off every male in Ahab's life, whether slave or freeman, in Israel. I will make your house like that of Jeroboam, son of Nebat, and like that of Baascha, son of Ahijah,

because of how you have provoked me by leading Israel into sin.' (Against Jezebel, too, the Lord declared, 'The dogs shall devour Jezebel in the district of Jezreel.') 'When one of Ahab's line dies, in the city, dogs will devour him; when one of them dies in the field, the birds of the sky will devour him.' Indeed, no one gave himself up to the doing of evil in the sight of the Lord as did Ahab, urged on by his wife Jezebel. He became completely abominable by following idols, just as the Amorites had done, whom the Lord drove out before the Israelites. When Ahab heard these words, he tore his garments and put on sackcloth over his bare flesh. He fasted, slept in the sackcloth, and went about subdued. Then the Lord said to Elijah the Tishbite, 'Have you seen that Ahab has humbled himself before me? Since he has humbled himself before me, I will not bring evil in his time. I will bring the evil upon his house during the reign of his son.' " (1 Kgs 21,20-29)*

"I turned to the Lord God, pleading in earnest prayer, with fasting, sackcloth, and ashes. I prayed to the Lord, my God and confessed, 'Ah, Lord, great and awesome God, you who keep your merciful covenant toward those who love you and observe your commandments! We have sinned, been wicked and done evil; we have rebelled and departed from your commandments and your laws.' " (Dn 9,3-5)

4.3. Fasting in a Time of Sorrow

"When the inhabitants of Jabesh-gilead heard what the Philistines had done to Saul, all their warriors set out, and after marching throughout the night, removed the bodies of Saul and his sons from the wall of Beth-shan, and brought them to Jabesh, where they cremated them. Then they took their bones and buried them under the tamarisk tree in Jabesh, and fasted for seven days." (1 Sm 31,11-13)

"David seized his garments and rent them, and all the men who were with him did likewise. They mourned and wept and fasted until evening for Saul and his son

Jonathan, and for the soldiers of the Lord of the clans of Israel, because they had fallen by the sword." (2 Sm 1,11-12)

"When all the inhabitants of Jabesh-gilead had heard what the Philistines had done to Saul, its warriors rose to a man, recovered the bodies of Saul and his sons, and brought them to Jabesh. They buried their bones under the oak of Jabesh, and fasted seven days." (1 Chr 10,11-12)

4.4. Prayer and Fasting for Healing

"Then David said to Nathan, 'I have sinned against the Lord.' Nathan answered David: 'The Lord on his part has forgiven your sin: you shall not die. But since you have utterly spurned the Lord by this deed, the child born to you must surely die.' Then Nathan returned to his house. The Lord struck the child that the wife of Uriah had borne to David, and it became desperately ill. David besought God for the child. He kept a fast, retiring for the night to lie on the ground clothed in sackcloth. The elders of his house stood beside him urging him to rise from the ground; but he would not, nor would he take food with them." (2 Sm 12,13-17)

4.5. Fasting and Inner Healing in an Experience with God

"He looked and there at his head was a hearth cake and a jug of water. After he ate and drank, he lay down again, but the angel of the Lord came back a second time, touched him and ordered, 'Get up and eat, else the journey will be too long for you!' He got up, ate and drank; then strengthened by that food, he walked forty days and forty nights to the mountain of God, Horeb.

There he came to a cave, where he took shelter. But the word of the Lord came to him, 'Why are you here, Elijah?' He answered: 'I have been most zealous for the Lord, the God of hosts, but the Israelites have forsaken your covenant, torn down the altars, and put your prophets to the sword. I alone am left, and they seek to take my life.'

Then the Lord said, 'Go outside and stand on the mountain before the Lord; the Lord will be passing by.' A strong and heavy wind was rending the mountains and crushing rocks before the Lord – but the Lord was not in the wind. After the wind, there was an earthquake - but the Lord was not in the earthquake. After the earthquake, there was fire - but the Lord was not in the fire. After the fire, there was a tiny whispering sound. When he heard this, Elijah hid his face in his cloak and went and stood at the entrance of the cave. A voice said to him, 'Elijah, why are you here.' "(1 Kgs 19,6-13)

4.6. Fasting and Danger of War

"The message was brought to Jehoshaphat: 'A great multitude is coming against you from across the sea, from Edom; they are already in Hazazontamar' (which is Engedi.) Johoshaphat was frightened, and he hastened to consult the Lord. He proclaimed a fast for all Judah. Then Judah gathered to seek help from the Lord; from every one of the cities of Judah they came to seek the Lord." (2 Chr 20,2-4)

"The altar, to, they draped in sackcloth; and with one accord they cried out fervently to the God of Israel not to allow their children to be seized, their wives to be taken captive, the cities of their inheritance to be ruined, or the sanctuary to be profaned and mocked for the nations to gloat over.

The Lord heard their cry and had regard for their distress. For the people observed a fast of many days' duration throughout Judea, and before the sanctuary of the Lord Almighty in Jerusalem." (Jdt 4,12-13)

"The assembly gathered together to prepare for battle and to pray and implore mercy and compassion. ... That day they fasted and wore sackcloth; they sprinkled ashes on their heads and tore their clothes." (1 Mc 3,44-47)

40

"When Judas learned of this, he urged the people to call upon the Lord night and day, to help them now, if ever, when they were about to be deprived of their law, their country, and their holy temple; and not to allow this nation, which had just begun to revive, to be subjected again to blasphemous Gentiles. When they had all joined in doing this, and had implored the merciful Lord continuously with weeping and fasting and prostrations for three days, Judas encouraged them and told them to stand ready." (2 Mc 13,10-12)

"Jonah began his journey through the city, and had gone but a single day's walk announcing, 'Forty days more and Nineveh shall be destroyed,' when the people of Nineveh believed God; they proclaimed a fast and all of them, great and small, put on sackcloth.

When the news reached the king of Nineveh, he rose from his throne, laid aside his robe, covered himself with sackcloth, and sat in the ashes. Then he had this proclaimed throughout Nineveh, by decree of the king and his nobles: 'Neither man nor beast, neither cattle nor sheep, shall taste anything; they shall not eat, nor shall they drink water. Man and beast shall be covered with sackcloth and call loudly to God; every man shall turn from his evil way and from the violence he has in hand. Who knows, God may relent and forgive, and withhold his blazing wrath, so that we shall not perish.'" (Jon 3,4-9)

4.7. Prayer and Fasting for a Blessing and a Safe Journey

"Then I proclaimed a fast, there by the river of Ahava, that we might humble ourselves before our God to petition from him a safe journey for ourselves, our children, and all our possessions. For I would have been ashamed to ask the king for troops and horsemen to protect us against our enemies along the way, since we had said to the king, 'The favoring hand of our God is upon all who seek him, but his mighty wrath is against all who forsake him.' So we fasted, and prayed to our

God for this, and our petition was granted." (Ezr 8,21-23)

4.8. Fasting after Destruction of War

". . .and they answered me: 'The survivors of the captivity there in the province are in great distress and under reproach. Also, the wall of Jerusalem lies breached, and its gates have been gutted with fire.' When I heard this report, I began to weep and continued mourning for several days; I fasted and prayed before the God of heaven." (Neh 1,3-4)

4.9. Fasting after Returning to the True God

"On the twenty-fourth day of this month, the Israelites gathered together fasting and in sackcloth, their heads covered with dust. Those of Israelite descent separated themselves from all who were of foreign extraction, then stood forward and confessed their sins and the guilty deeds of their fathers." (Neh 9,1-2)

4.10. Fasting, Prayer, Almsgiving and Righteousness

"Prayer and fasting are good, but better than either almsgiving accompanied by righteousness. A little with righteousness is better than abundance with wickedness. It is better to give alms than to store up gold." (Tob 12,8)

4.11. Life-long Fasting out of Sorrow

". . .where she set up a tent for herself on the roof of her house. She put sackcloth about her loins and wore widow's weeds. She fasted all the days of her widowhood, except Sabbath eves and Sabbaths, new moon eves and new moons, feast days and holidays of the house of Israel." (Jdt 8,5-6)

"There was a prophetess, Anna, the daughter of Phanuel, of the tribe of Asher. She was advanced in years, having lived seven years with her husband after

her marriage and then as a widow until she was eighty-four. She never left the temple, but worshipped night and day with fasting and prayer. And coming forward at that very time, she gave thanks to God and spoke about the child to all who were awaiting the redemption of Jerusalem." (Lk 2,36-38)

4.12. Fasting in a Situation Endangering the People

At the advice of Haman, King Ahasuerus gave a proclamation against the Jewish nation. When people found out about the danger facing them, this is how they reacted:

"When Mordecai learned all that was happening, he tore his garments, put on sackcloth and ashes, and walked through the city, crying out loudly and bitterly; till he came before the royal gate, which no one clothed in sackcloth might enter. (Likewise in each of the provinces, wherever the king's legal enactment reached, the Jews went into deep mourning, with fasting, weeping, and lament; they all slept on sackcloth and ashes.)

Esther sent back to Mordecai the response; 'Go and assemble all the Jews who are in Susa; fast on my behalf, all of you, not eating and drinking, night or day, for three days. I and my maids will also fast in the same way. Thus prepared, I will to go to the king, contrary to the law. If I perish, I perish!'

Queen Esther, seized with mortal anguish, likewise had recourse to the Lord. Taking off her splendid garments, she put on garments of distress and mourning. In place of her precious ointments she covered her head with dirt and ashes. She afflicted her body severely; all her festive adornments were put aside, and her hair was wholly disheveled. Then she prayed to the Lord, the God of Isreal . . ." (Est 4,1-3,15,16; 4C,12g,14)

4.13. Fasting in Psalms

"But I, when they were ill, put on sackcloth, I afflicted myself with fasting and poured forth prayers within my bosom." (Ps 35,13)

"I humbled myself with fasting, and this was made a reproach to me. I made sackcloth my garment, and I became a byword for them." (Ps 69,11-12)

"My knees totter from my fasting, and my flesh is wasted of its substance. And I have become a mockery to them; when they see me, they shake their heads." (Ps 109,24-25)

"So with a man who fasts for his sins, but then goes and commits them again: Who will hear his prayer, and what has he gained by his mortification?" (Sir 34,26)

4.14. The Meaning of Fasting – a New Relationship

"Cry out full-throated and unsparingly, lift up your voice like a trumpet blast; Tell my people their wickedness, and the house of Jacob their sins.

They seek me day after day, and desire to know my ways, Like a nation that has done what is just and not abandoned the law of their God; They ask me to declare what is due them, pleased to gain access to God.

"Why do we fast, and you do not see it? afflict ourselves, and you take no note of it?" Lord, on your fast day you carry out your own pursuits, and drive all your laborers.

Yes, your fast ends in quarreling and fighting, striking with wicked claw. Would that today you might fast so as to make your voice heard on high!

Is this the manner of fasting I wish, of keeping a day of penance: That a man bow his head like a reed, and lie in sackcloth and ashes? Do you call this a fast, a day acceptable to the Lord?

This, rather, is the fasting that I wish: releasing those bound unjustly untying the thongs of the yoke; setting free the oppressed, breaking every yoke." (Is 58,1-6)

Then the Lord said to me: "Do not intercede for this people. If they fast, I will not listen to their supplication. If they offer holocausts or cereal offerings, I will not accept them. Rather, I will destroy them with the sword, famine, and pestilence." (Jer 14,11-12)

"Thereupon this word of the Lord of hosts came to me: Say to all the people of the land and to the priests; When you fasted and mourned in the fifth and in the seventh month these seventy years, was it really for me that you fasted?" (Zeh 7,4-5)

"This word of the Lord of hosts came to me: Thus says the Lord of hosts: The fast days of the fourth, the fifth, the seventh, and tenth months shall become occasions of joy and gladness, cheerful festivals for the house of Judah; only love, faithfulness and peace." (Zed 8,18-19)

4.15. Fasting and Preparation for Listening to the Word of God

"In the ninth month, in the fifth year of Jehoiakim, son of Josiah, king of Judah, a fast to placate the Lord was proclaimed for all the people of Jerusalem and all who came from Judah's cities to Jerusalem. Then Jeremiah charged Baruch: I cannot go to the house of the Lord; I am prevented from doing so. Do you go on the fast day and read publicly in the Lord's house the Lord's words from the scroll you wrote at my dictation; read them also to all the men of Judah who come up from their cities. Perhaps they will lay their supplication before the Lord and will all turn back from their evil way; for great is the fury of anger with which the Lord has threatened this people." (Jer 36,9;5-7)

4.16. Responding to the Word of God with Prayer and Fasting

"And Baruch read the words of this scroll for Jeconiah, son of Jehoiakim, king of Judah, to hear it, as well as all the people who came to the readings; the nobles, the king's sons, the elders, and the whole people, small and

great alike—all who lived in Babylon by the river Sud. They wept and fasted and prayed before the Lord and collected such funds as each could furnish." (Bar 1,3-6)

4.17. Fasting and Prayer as a Way out of a Common Sinful State

"Gird yourselves and weep, O priests! wail, O ministers of the altar! Come, spend the night in sackcloth, O ministers of my God! The house of your God is deprived of offering and libation. Proclaim a fast, call an assembly; Gather the elders, all who dwell in the land, Into the house of the Lord, your God, and cry to the Lord." (Jl 1,13-14)

"Yet, even now, says the Lord, return to me with your whole heart, with fasting, and weeping, and mourning; Rend your hearts, not your garments, and return to the Lord, your God. For gracious and merciful is he, slow to anger, rich in kindness, and relenting in punishment. Perhaps he will again relent and leave behind him a blessing, Offering and libations for the Lord your God. Blow the trumpet in Zion! proclaim a fast, call an assembly. . ." (Jl 2,12-15)

THE NEW TESTAMENT

4.18. Jesus' Fast

Then Jesus was led by the Spirit unto the desert to be tempted by the devil. He fasted for forty days and forty nights, and afterwards he was hungry. The tempter approached and said to him, "If you are the Son of God, command that these stones become loaves of bread." He said in reply, "It is written: 'One does not live by bread alone, but by every word that comes forth from the mouth of God.'"

Then the devil took him to the holy city, and made him stand on the parapet of the temple, and said to him, "If you are the Son of God, throw yourself down. For it is written: 'He will command his angels concerning you, and with their hands they will support you, lest you dash your foot against a stone.' "

Jesus answered him, "Again it is written, You shall not put the Lord your God, to the test." Then the devil took him up to a very high mountain, and showed him all the kingdoms of the world in their magnificence, and he said to him, "All these I shall give to you, if you will prostrate yourself and worship me." At this Jesus said to him, "Get away, Satan!" It is written: 'The Lord your God shall you worship and him alone shall you serve.'

Then the devil left him and, behold angels came and ministered to him." (Mt 4,1-11)

Jesus and Adam

Jesus' temptation in the desert took place before the beginning of his public life. Jesus goes into the desert and there he prays and fasts.

The first temptation pertains to material things. The second consists of a suggestion that Jesus test the Father. He is to find out if God, whom he calls Father, will do anything to prevent him from being hurt if he jumps. In other words, if man does something that leads to ruin, will God respond to such a provocation? Jesus refuses to put God to the test. He warns that God must not be tested, rather that the law that God himself has placed in nature must be upheld.

The third temptation is one of power. Jesus is to worship Satan who would then give Him a reward: power. Jesus rejects every temptation. Only then do the angels come and minister to Him.

It is not by chance that St. Matthew understands and portrays the beginning of Jesus' public life particularly in this way. Jesus came to rectify the sin of Adam and Eve. They had everything, but lost it because they became blind to what they had, and opened their eyes to what was forbidden to them - what they did not have. In reaching for what was forbidden, they wanted what did not belong to them. In this way, they lost everything and had to go into a desert in their relationship with God and with each other. All at once, they found themselves in a desert because they had to leave Heaven - the harmonious relationship between God, man and nature.

Jesus came to save everyone, to renew the world that had fallen, and to open the way of salvation to it. He had to go into the 'desert' as a consequence of sin for the new world to begin, the world of the Kingdom of God. Thus, He opened the new way to man – the way of salvation. After He refused to reach for what was forbidden, as Adam and Eve did, the angels came (a sign of reinstated Heaven of the Kingdom of God) and they ministered to Him.

In this way, Jesus personally entered into the new kingdom and opened the way of salvation to everyone, whereas it had been lost for all. This process is true for all mankind. Often when man has everything, he loses everything because, in comfort, God is easily forgotten; man stops being cognizant of His presence. Only when man loses God, does he start to really look for Him, because the desert of man's relationship with God is unbearable to man.

The image of man is clear in this. He can have peace and experience happiness only when he has overcome his desert (when he has overcome materialism, hunger for glory and power and every testing of God) and has abandoned his life completely to God.

Because fasting was so important in Jesus' life and was a condition for the opening of God's way, we, too, must discover the same meaning of fasting. A person who fasts enters into his desert where he decides again for God. In this decision for God, the new world begins, the world of God's Kingdom.

The new world cannot be reinstated if man does not go into the desert where he can more easily recognize evil and the evil one and, where he can successfully fight for the good.

4.19. Jesus Speaks about Fasting

"When you fast, do not look gloomy like the hypocrites. They neglect their appearance, so that they may appear to others to be fasting. Amen I say to you, they have received their reward. But when you fast, anoint your head and wash your face, so that you may not appear to be fasting, except to your Father who is hidden. And your Father who sees what is hidden will repay you." (Mt 6,16-18)

"Two people went up to the temple area to pray; one was a Pharisee and the other was a tax collector. The Pharisee took up his position and spoke this prayer to himself, 'O God, I thank you that I am not like the rest of humanity –- greedy, dishonest, adulterous – or even like this tax collector. I fast twice a week, and I pay tithes on my whole income.' But the tax collector stood off at a distance and would not even raise his eyes to heaven but beat his breast and prayed, 'O God, be merciful to me a sinner.' I tell you, the latter went home justified, not the former; for everyone who exalts himself will be humbled, and the one who humbles himself will be exalted." (Lk 18,10-14)

4.20. Jesus' Disciples will Fast

"Then the disciples of John approached him and said, "Why do we and the Pharisees fast (much), but your disciples do not fast?" Jesus answered them, "Can the wedding guests mourn as long as the bridegroom is with them? The days will come when the bridegroom is taken away from them, and then they will fast." " (Mt 9,14-15)

The disciples of John and of the Pharisees were accustomed to fast. People came to him and objected, "Why do the disciples of John and the disciples of the Pharisees fast, but your disciples do not fast?" Jesus answered them, "Can the wedding guests fast while the bridegroom is with them? As long as they have the bridegroom with them they cannot fast. But the days will come when the bridegroom is taken away from them, and then they will fast on that day." (Mk 2,18-20)

"And they said to him, "The disciples of John fast often and offer prayers, and the disciples of the Pharisees do the same; but yours eat and drink." Jesus answered them, "Can you make the wedding guests fast while the bridegroom is with them?" But the days will come, and when the bridegroom is taken away from them, then they will fast in those days." (Lk 5,33–35)

4.21. Fasting and Prayer Strengthen Faith

He said to them, "Because of your little faith. Amen, I say to you, if you have faith the size of a mustard seed, you will say to this mountain, 'Move from here to there,' and it will move. Nothing will be impossible for you. But this kind does not come out except by prayer and fasting." (Mt 2,20-21)

4.22. Fasting and Prayer Used Against Satan

Jesus, on seeing a crowd rapidly gathering, rebuked the unclean spirit and said to it, "Mute and deaf spirit, I command you: come out of him and never enter him again!" Shouting and throwing the boy into convulsions, it came out. He became like a corpse, which caused many to say, "He is dead!" But Jesus took him by the hand, raised him, and he stood up. When he entered the house, his disciples asked him in private, "Why could we not drive it out?" He said to them, "This kind can only come out through prayer and fasting." [3] (Mk 9,25-29)

4.23. Fasting and Prayer Before Being Sent to Serve

"While they were worshiping the Lord and fasting, the Holy Spirit said, "Set apart for me Barnabas and Saul for the work to which I have called them" Then, completing their fasting and prayer, they laid hands on them and sent them off." (Acts 13,2-3)

---

[3] The word fasting has been omitted in certain translations.

"After they had proclaimed the good news to that city and made a considerable number of disciples, they returned to Lystra and to Iconium and to Antioch. They strengthened the spirits of the disciples and exhorted them to persevere in the faith, saying, "It is necessary for us to undergo many hardships to enter the kingdom of God." They appointed presbyters for them in each church and, with prayer and fasting, commended them to the Lord in whom they had put their faith." (Acts 14,21-23)

4.24. St. Paul Fasts

"We cause no one to stumble in anything, in order that no fault may be found with our ministry; on the contrary, in everything we commend ourselves as ministers of God, through much endurance, in afflictions, hardships, constraints, beatings, imprisonments, riots, labors, vigils, fasts; by purity, knowledge, patience, kindness, in a holy spirit, in unfeigned love, in truthful speech, in the power of God; with weapons of righteousness at the right and at the left; through glory and dishonor, insult and praise. We are treated as deceivers and yet are truthful; . . ." (2 Cor 6,3-8)

"Three times I was beaten with rods, once I was stoned, three times I was shipwrecked, I passed a night and a day on the deep; on frequent journeys, in dangers from rivers, dangers from robbers, dangers from my own race, dangers from Gentiles, dangers in the city, dangers in the wilderness, dangers at sea, dangers among false brothers; in toil and hardship, through many sleepless nights, through hunger and thirst, through frequent fastings, through cold and exposure." (2 Cor 11,25-28)

4.25. Eschatology Dimension of Fasting

A Christian follows Christ. Christ is a pilgrim who came to meet man threatened by the danger of being lost, of wondering astray or of stopping on the way. Since coming to meet him, man's journey and life became a pilgrimage and everything has turned to the good. Jesus accompanies man - He is the Way, the Truth, the Life, the Light and Nutrition for him.

By nature, man is a pilgrim who seeks God in everything as an answer to his questions. It is not good for him to permit himself to be imprisoned or stopped on the way by anything of this world. That is why, he must remain free. He must not permit himself to be imprisoned by the world to become an addict. When a Christian decides to, and does, fast he witnesses to his faith in the ultimate reality that lasts forever. To fast means to free himself from things of this world and not to permit worldly realities to cloud his sight of what is eternal.

Even a cursory look at the Biblical revelation is sufficient in order to see how often human and sacred feasts are spoken of. We find over 80 citing's of feasts, in various situations, in the Bible. In the New Testament, we see reference to Christ's feasts and the eschatological feast. In the Old Testament, the Paschal feast is the most familiar in commemoration of the wondrous love with which God intervened for the Israelites and led them out of Egypt. The Israelites were told everything about this feast which none of them was permitted to, or could, forget. (Cf. Ex 12 and 13)

"On the tenth of this month every one of your families must procure for itself a lamb, one apiece for each household. If a family is too small for a whole lamb, it shall join the nearest household in procuring one and shall share in the lamb in proportion to the number of person who partake of it. The lamb must be a year old male and without blemish." (Ex 12,3-5)

Even the way the lamb was to be eaten was clearly set out:

"This is how you are to eat it: with your loins girt, sandals on your feet and your staff in your hand, you shall eat like those who are in flight. It is the Passover of the Lord." (Ex 12,11)

Along with the reality of this feast in its historical context, it is also eschatological in its meaning because it is a symbol of the Eucharist feast. Jesus eats the Paschal feast with His disciples and gives the gift of the Eucharist. He is the Lamb of God giving Himself not only for the life of the Israelite nation but also for the entire world. (cf. Lk 22,7-18. . .)

The feast of which the prophet Isaiah speaks of in Chapter 25 is eschatological in its own way:

"On this mountain the Lord of hosts will provide for all peoples, a feast of rich food and choice wines, juicy, rich food and pure, choice wines. On this mountain, he will destroy the veil that veils all peoples. The web that is woven over all nations; he will destroy death forever. The Lord God will wipe away the tears from all faces; the reproach of his people he will remove from the whole earth; for the Lord has spoken. On that day it will be said: 'behold our God, to whom we looked to save us! This is the Lord for whom we looked; let us rejoice and be glad that he has saved us!' For the hand of the Lord will rest on this mountain. . ." (Is 25,6-10)

Jesus spoke about the Kingdom of God in images and parables, often speaking about feasts. He also spoke about the eternal feast of the Kingdom of God. St. Luke notes His words:

"It is you who have stood by me in my trials; and I confer a kingdom on you, just as my Father has conferred one on me, that you may eat and drink at my table in my kingdom; and you will sit on thrones judging the twelve tribes of Israel." (Lk 22,28-30)

After establishing the Eucharist, Jesus said:

"I tell you, from now on I shall not drink this fruit of the vine until the day when I drink it with you new in the kingdom of my Father." (Mt 26,29)

This feast is to be together with the forefathers of the faith:

"I say to you, many will come from the east and the west, and will recline with Abraham, Isaac, and Jacob at the banquet in the kingdom of heaven, but the children of the kingdom will be driven out into the outer darkness, where there will be wailing and grinding of teeth." (Mt 8,11-12)

There are also conditions for partaking in the feast:

"The kingdom of heaven may be likened to a king who gave a wedding feast for his son. He dispatched his servants to summon the invited guests to the feast, but they refused to come. . . But when the king came in to meet the guests he saw a man there not dressed in a wedding garment. He said to him, 'My friend, how is it that you came in here without a wedding garment?' " (Mt 22,2-3; 11-12)

The feast is being prepared. Everyone is called, but not everyone responds. Among those who do respond, not all are prepared to partake.

Jesus speaks about waiting for the Groom because the feast can only begin when the Groom arrives. The behavior and final results vary. The virgins waited for the Groom to enter the feast with Him. Because He was late, they fell asleep. Five of them entered the wedding feast because they had oil in their lanterns and five were called foolish because they were not prepared to enter. (cf. Mt 25,1+)

It is necessary to be awake and to wait. If the servant concludes that the master will be late and he is no longer prepared to wait (namely, if he loses the dimension of waiting and of being turned toward the future) he turns toward himself, to eating and to drinking. Misunderstanding, conflicts and wars then take place. (cf. Mt 24,45+)

Fasting makes man capable of waiting - not to grow tired of waiting. At the same time, fasting becomes a direct witness to the expectation of the eternal feast in the Kingdom of God. Everything written in the book of Revelations will be accomplished.

"Behold, I stand at the door and knock. If anyone hears my voice and opens the door, [then] I will enter his house and dine with him, and he with me." (Rv 3,20)

4.26. Bread and Water – Pilgrim's Food

In the first place, the call to a life with bread and water is a call of preparation for the meeting with Christ in the Eucharist. At the same time, this call wants to increase our awareness of our life's pilgrim journey on earth. Man's entire life and all of his activity can be seen from the standpoint of a pilgrimage.

Through the history of man's thought, and especially in the past decades, frequent theories have proclaimed man to be a wanderer on this earth – as not knowing where he comes from or where he is going. The Christian standpoint pertaining to man is completely different. In his essence and according to his nature, man seeks God. In himself, he bears questions about eternal life, happiness and peace and the answer to these questions is God. Man does not wander about aimlessly. He journeys towards his fullness and the final truth about himself, which he can only realize in God. This is why man, in himself, is a pilgrim. A pilgrim, in turn, is someone who leaves his daily life, work, security and joy and goes on a journey towards individuals and places where he can meet God more easily - where God has revealed Himself in a special way.

In the past there were no modern means facilitating quick and easy transport from one place to another. Pilgrimages lasted for weeks, months and even years. A pilgrim was only able to bring with him the basic necessities of life: bread and water; and this is what he did. Leaving behind his daily life and going on a journey with a bag on his shoulders containing bread and water, he freed himself of all burdens and every excess. Free in this way, he was able to go on to individuals and places where he sought to meet God. These places, however, were only points of passage from which he proceeded further or returned to his daily life. Even his return to everyday life did not stop portraying the characteristics of a pilgrimage because a person does not have a permanent residence in this world. He is on a pilgrimage towards the eternal homeland of complete peace and joy, eternal life and unity.

Today, by living on bread and water, man retains his freedom. He does not become a slave to material things or a victim of false promises. In his freedom, he is prepared to love, to forgive, to overcome conflicts and to live in peace. Whenever man forgets his pilgrim journey, he stops on the way and destroys himself in anxious concerns of this world.

God also gave man the Heavenly Bread. He gave His Son Who by His presence has become man's continuous companion on his pilgrimage. This is why the Messiah's name is Emmanuel, meaning 'God with us'. God journeys with man as Bread, that is the life to the world. When a believer forgets that his God journeys with him in the form of Bread, he turns to the world where he can never feel well, without being turned towards God.

In this context, the final meaning of fasting is found. Fasting is not only a means of healing, calming and freeing. Together with prayer and charity, it is a fundamental means to a religious experience; namely, to an awareness of the truth about oneself and for opening oneself to God, Who has decided completely for man.

4.27. The Forgotten Fast

When we become aware of the Biblical practice of fasting, (in both the Old and New Testaments) of the Church tradition and of the experience of saints of the Catholic Church; in contrast to what is left of fasting in our time, we can rightly say: "FASTING HAS BEEN FORGOTTEN." Anselm Grün wrote:

"Where is there fasting today? Barely where we expect it the most, in monasteries. There, many reasons are given why it is not possible to fast today as St. Benedict envisioned in his rule or as St. Francis practised: that today it is necessary to work more than before, that it is no longer healthy and that much depends on the period of time." [4]

According to Church law, only two days of fasting remain: Ash Wednesday and Good Friday. If the recommendation is followed of eating once until satisfied and less for two other meals, then it can be said that fasting does not exist at all. Every reasonable person should always eat one meal a day until full and less at two other meal times. Anything more is not good for the human organism.

Friday used to be a day when Christians did not eat meat. This has also become a matter of a personal choice and is truly a great loss both for spiritual and physical health. Fasting in preparation for feast days has also been lost.

Recently what is being said about fasting shows that even its meaning has been completely lost. According to legal interpretation, fasting can be replaced by good works or by some sacrifice or renunciation. This is entirely wrong. Whoever can fast cannot replace fasting with anything else, just as a person who is sick cannot substitute his participation at Holy Mass with any other prayer. Somebody who is sick is justified in not participating at Mass but still cannot replace Holy Mass with prayer. For example, when someone says they are renouncing cigarettes or alcohol for Lent, this is good, but it is not fasting. It is also worthy to do good works, but this, too, does not replace fasting.

First of all, fasting and prayer are a means to an inner cleansing and freeing. Secondly they are a condition for

---

[4] Grün, Anselm, OSB, *Fasten*, Vier–Türme-Verlag, Münsterschwarzach, 1984. , p. 55.

proper spiritual growth and a proper disposition towards oneself, others, nature and God.

4.28. Everyone is called To Fast

We must not forget that the healthy and the sick, the young and the old, the rich and the poor, the holy and the sinful must all fast; although, the consequences of their fasting certainly differ. By means of their fasting and prayer, the healthy will have more compassion for the sick. The sick will more easily endure their cross and, as many have experienced, they will get well more easily.

By fasting and prayer the young will retain their freedom and will not permit bad habits to imprison them. They will recognize them more easily and will overcome them more successfully. By fasting and prayer the elderly will more easily retain peace and live their days with greater joy. They will be more generous and grateful for their lives.

By fasting and prayer the rich will comprehend what they need and what they have. In this way, they will be able more easily to share their goods with their poor brothers. Fasting and prayer will help them not to become proud in their wealth and will protect them from unjust behavior. Fasting and prayer will help them to be grateful for what they have.

By fasting and prayer the poor will more easily carry their cross of poverty and will not fall into the temptation of thinking that they will have everything when they have more, or when they become rich. Fasting will protect them from becoming bitter in their poverty.

Fasting and prayer will help a sinner to understand his sinfulness more easily; to acknowledge his responsibility better; to repent more sincerely; and to receive the strength to free himself from evil and sin.

By fasting and prayer those who are holy will grow in love, faith, hope, abandonment and trust in God.

By fasting and prayer, it is also easier to protect the environment. There would be less garbage; and we would be able to overcome the general world danger of rapidly using up all natural resources as if we were the last generation on earth.

As you read this book, the third Millennium is constantly spoken of and questions are being asked as to what it will bring us. A better question to ask is: 'What are we like as we enter into the third Millennium?' If we rush into the new Millennium with our pride, greed, insatiable appetite for food and drink and a tireless race for material goods, we will continually cause adversity. We will collide against each other in selfishness and greed destroying the family unit, the Church, the community and the world in general.

To restore fasting and prayer in the Biblical sense means to create conditions for a new life.

FASTING MUST NO LONGER BE FORGOTTEN AND MISUNDERSTOOD. IT MUST BE RESTORED AND REGAIN ITS PROPER PLACE - FOR OUR SAKE, FOR THE SAKE OF NATURE, FOR THE SAKE OF OTHERS, AND FINALLY FOR THE SAKE OF OUR RELATIONSHIP WITH GOD!

A Canadian Benedictine, Adalbert de Vogue, in his book, 'To Love Fasting' admits that Medjugorje's call to fasting has helped the Church return to the practice of fasting.

"Specifically, religious fasting has not completely disappeared. The recent apparitions of the Virgin of Medjugorje have even restored to honor the ancient observance of fasting on bread and water on Wednesday and Friday. But western Christianity remains deprived of living customs and spiritual motives . . ." [5]

---

[5] Vogüe, Adalbert de, *To Love Fasting, The Monastic Experience*, Petersham, MA 01366, p. 38.

V. CATECHISM OF THE CATHOLIC CHURCH ON FASTING

In the newest Catechism of the Catholic Church, it is easy to recognize the actual standpoint on fasting. In looking at the fundamental Biblical, theologically-moral themes according to the space allotted to them, it can be seen that fasting has lost its place, its meaning, and especially its practice. While, justifiably, some 70 pages are dedicated to the theme of prayer, fasting is only mentioned in passing in nine places.

In number 575, fasting is mentioned for the first time and only in parenthesis when forms of piety are noted: "almsgiving, fasting and prayer."

In number 1387, fasting is mentioned to prepare for worthy reception of the sacrament of Holy Communion, but only according to the requirements of the local Church. There is nothing specific said about what this preparation consists of, how long it is to last or what its real meaning is.

In number 1430, it is said that Jesus' "call to conversion and penance, like that of the prophets before him does not aim first at outward works, 'sackcloth and ashes, fasting and mortification', but at the conversion of the heart, interior conversion." In this, it is stressed that penitential acts are sterile and false without the interior conversion of the heart.

A clear relationship between outward works and the interior state of the heart and soul is already found with the prophets. This seems to be completely forgotten. An injustice is committed against the proclamation of the prophets in this and Jesus' word is placed in such a context as to make fasting in itself unnecessary. It is not possible to avoid the impression that there is a danger of looking at fasting superficially. Conversion of the heart is a fruit of fasting and prayer, as well as for their correctness. Fasting and prayer always remain closely interconnected just like grades and studying are in school. In the above statement, there is an impression that the grade is more important than the studying. Although it is true that the grade is important because without it, studying would have no meaning, nonetheless, in order to receive the grade one has to study.

In number 1434, it is stressed that "interior penance of the Christian can be expressed in 'many and different ways' namely fasting, prayer and almsgiving, which express conversion in relation to oneself, to God and to others." Fasting, prayer and almsgiving are means through which forgiveness of sins, reconciliation with one's neighbor and an act of love towards one's neighbor is received.

Even in this is it not possible to avoid an impression of superficiality because we recall that when Jesus fasted it was not for any of the above-noted reasons. Fasting has a profound sense that is never lost regardless of what situation man finds himself in. The rich, the poor, the holy and the sinful must all fast and pray because fasting and prayer are fundamental conditions for, and expressions of, a relationship with God, with oneself and with others.

In number 1438, seasons and days of penance in the course of the liturgical year are mentioned: Lent and each Friday. These times are noted as particularly appropriate for "spiritual exercises, penitential liturgies and pilgrimages as signs of penance." Fasting is introduced as "voluntary self-denial" for the benefit of one's neighbor.

If it is the intention of the Catechism to introduce the complete Revelation, tradition and practice of the Church, then this is not sufficient. However, if the Catechism only conveys conclusions on the basis of today's practice, then enough is said. According to today's practice in the Church, fasting is almost non-existent.

In 1755, fasting is again mentioned in parenthesis as an example of an action that has no value if it is not carried out with the right intention, namely, if one fasts 'in order to be seen by men.'

In this context, if we speak about fasting, it is possible to conclude that it is more dangerous to fast in order to be seen by others, than to eat and drink excessively before them.

Number 1969, notes that "The New Law practices the acts of religion: almsgiving, prayer and fasting" directing them to the Father who sees the intentions of the heart.

From experience a question is asked, How can there be true intentions of the heart at all without fasting and prayer? Just as the danger of fasting, as an external action must not be overemphasized, it is not just to overemphasize the intention that inspires fasting and to which fasting leads. They must always be seen in terms of a means and a goal. A goal is not reached without the means and the means has no meaning without the goal.

In number 2043, there is only a mention that fasting "prepares us for the liturgical feasts and helps us acquire mastery over our instincts and freedom of heart."

With fasting and prayer, freedom of heart really is achieved and through it, man more successfully battles against every evil in himself and around him. Particularly because of this fasting is important.

In number 2742, there is a citation from the works of *Capita practica ad Anatolium, Evagrius Ponticus*, which pertains to the requirement to pray without ceasing: "For we have not been commanded to work, to keep watch and to fast constantly, but it has been laid down that we are to pray without ceasing." [6]

---

[6] Respective paragraph numbers are from *The Catechism of the Catholic Church*, Veritas, Dublin, 1994

Practice confirms the truth that when a person fasts he prays better, and when he prays he fasts better and easier.

Perhaps we must also say here: what God has joined together let no man separate!

VI. A HISTORICAL LOOK AT THE TWO DAY FAST

6.1. From Jewish To Christian Practice

In the history of the Church, the practice of the two-day fast has its roots in the Jewish tradition. As far as it is possible to look back, it can be said that the two-day practice of fasting from Judaism found a place very early in the practice of the Church. While Jews fasted on Mondays and Thursdays, in the history of the Church, Wednesdays and Fridays were fast days. The days of fasting were substituted for justifiable reasons - Fridays because of the death of Jesus on the Cross and Wednesdays in reparation for all sins and offenses. According to one tradition, it was on Wednesday evening of Holy Week that Judas went to the Pharisees and made the deal with them – when, for how much money, where and how he was to betray Jesus.

6.2. Gaelic Names for Weekdays Pertaining to Fasting

The practice of the two-day fast found an interesting position in Ireland where the Church, in the beginning, was very strong. In particular, many missionaries in Western Europe, including St. Columbanus, St. Gaul and others, came from Ireland. The two-day practice of fasting left its mark in the Gaelic names for the days of the week. Wednesday – *Ceadaoin* - means the 'first fast,' Thursday – *Daordaoin* – means 'between fasts,' and Friday – *Aoine* – means 'the fast.'

In order to understand the importance of this as proof of the existence of a two-day fast in Ireland, we recall that the names of days in Slavic languages came about by simple numeration. *Ponedjeljak* (Monday) is the 'day after Sunday,' *srijeda* (Wednesday) means the 'middle of the week,' *četvrtak* (Thursday) is the 'fourth day' and *petak* (Friday) is the 'fifth day.' In Latin, Roman and

Germanic languages, the names of days have their roots in the Greco-Roman and other mythologies: *Martes – martedi – mardi* is the day of the god of war, *Venerdi – venredi* is the day of *Venere*, *Donnerstag* is the day of the god of thunder, etc.

VII. FASTING IN THE LIVES OF SAINTS

It is known that saints prayed and fasted. In the rules of all Orders, Wednesdays and Fridays are special days of fasting. Extended periods of fasting such as during Lent are also prescribed. Unfortunately, according to the testimonies I have collected, fasting has been forsaken even in the strictest Monastic orders.

There are instances of individuals known in the Church, such as St. Nicholas von Flüe, Theresa Neuman, and, more recently, Martha Robin, who lived only on the Eucharist. Those are special graces given by the Lord. They lived solely on Heavenly Bread by which the Father confirms the words of His Son in an exceptional way: *'I am the bread of life; whoever comes to me will never hunger.'* (Jn 6,35)

Although I do not intend to expound individually on the fasting of particular saints, I shall at least touch on what St. Benedict and St. Francis did.

7.1. Saint Benedict

St. Benedict is the father of Western Monasticism. In his rule of life and the practice of his sons, fasting occupied a very important place for a long time. They fasted during Lent eating only once a day or only two or three days in a week, depending on the period of time. St. Benedict's words became the golden rule: "To love fasting!"

All other virtues become possible through fasting, especially the virtue of chastity. St. Benedict spoke the same words he spoke about fasting, only in reference to chastity: "To love chastity!" He saw a profound connection between fasting and chastity. For a religious to be pure means to renounce carnal union completely and to conquer it. This can only be done if there is a renunciation of the enjoyment of food by means of fasting. For this reason, religious must love fasting and chastity, because by it they renounce themselves and open themselves to a profound union with God. In this way, they become capable of loving God and their neighbor as Christ calls us to. Fasting purifies the soul and the body and gives joy and freedom to the entire being. Although this is not easy, whoever puts this into practice will experience, in his own life, that it is good to fast.[7]

Over time, fasting started to disappear in the Church generally, in the monastic life and even among the Benedictines.

Adalbert de Vogüe in his fore mentioned book, *To Love Fasting* attests that the Benedictine monasteries no longer fast and that the Benedictines grant themselves all three meals. He found only one Benedictine community in Abiquiu, New Mexico, that fasts in the way that Saint Benedict prescribed. That community lives in extreme poverty, far from all civilization. The brothers live from their work and pray seven times a day.

Many reasons are cited for fasting being forgotten, but there is no sufficient reason to neglect the practice of the Church and the Monastic practice.[8]

7.2. Saint Francis of Assisi

With his life being a reflection of the Gospel, St. Francis has remained a great inspiration for many, especially the young. This is true not only for Catholic Orders but also for other Christian communities. Even non-Christians accept him as a man who enraptures and inspires them. Christian tradition acknowledges that he became most like Christ during his life. The reason for this is not only in the fact that on September 17, 1225, St. Francis received the wounds of Christ on his body. It is also because of his whole way of life and his relationship with others, with nature and with God. *The*

---

[7] Vogüe, *To Love Fasting*, p. 127.
[8] *Ibid.*, p.67.

Canticle of Creation is a great expression of his love for creatures and for God Who is the Creator of all.

In this way Francis, by his example, enraptured others with his life, inspired, and called them to change their lives. He did this as per the age-old rule which states that saints are not only here for us to be in awe of them, but for us to follow them. Not only are they our intercessors, they are also a concrete call for us to follow them.

Certainly, it is much easier to remain in admiration of them than to imitate them. Even St. Francis did not become what he was without a profound reason: he prayed and fasted. Francis prayed much and was called "pure prayer", but he also fasted much. In the Admonitions, "The Regula Bullata" Chapter 3 it is written:

"And let them fast from the Feast of All Saints until the Nativity of the Lord. Indeed the holy lent, which begins from Epiphany throughout the forty following days, which the Lord consecrated by His own holy fast (Mt 4:2), let those who voluntarily fast it be blest by the Lord, and let those who do not want (to do so) not be constrained. But let them fast the other (lent) until the Resurrection of the Lord. However at other times let them not be bound to fast, except on Fridays." [9]

In addition to these forty-day fasts, it is known that St. Francis fasted yet another forty days before the feast of St. Michael the Archangel on Sept 29. During such a fast, he received the wounds of Christ on Mt. LaVerna and in this way, became completely Christ like. In the Admonitions, "The Regula Non-Bullata" it is written:

"And similarly let every friar fast from the Feast of All Saints until Christmas and from Epiphany, when Our Lord Jesus Christ began to fast, until Easter." [10] In this

---

[9] *The Complete Writing of St. Francis and St. Clare*. New Text Edition. Editiones Collegii, Grottaferrata, (Rome) 1976. p. 11. (Translated from the Latin Critical Edition by Fr. K. Esser, O.F.M.).
[10] *Ibid.*, p. 5-7.

unconfirmed rule, the forty-day fast, beginning at Epiphany is not left to choice as it is in the confirmed rule.

Whoever is enthused by St. Francis's example does not only want to remain in admiration of him, but wants to start to fast and pray more. Through fasting and prayer one opens himself to the grace of God and continues to become similar to Christ. Through fasting and prayer, inner freedom is achieved and only in such freedom, can one grow in love and discover the beauty of life and of God's creatures. Only then is it possible to forgive and even to endure difficulties joyfully and with love. Only then is it possible to call death one's 'sister' and welcome it.

Francis's relationship with nature especially inspires us at this time when we witness how endangered it is. An increasing number of ecological movements to protect nature are being organized to save man's environment and by that, to save man himself. Whenever we intervene for creatures, we also express our love and respect for the Creator.

7.3. Brief Texts about Fasting from the Traditional Church

Aristides wrote about King **Hadrian** and about the first Christians:

While there are the poor among them in need of help, they fast two or three days and then ordinarily send them the food they had for themselves.

Pastor Hermes (about year 150):

During that day of fasting, you will not take anything other than bread and water. Then you will calculate the amount you would have used for food and give it to a widow, an orphan or the poor. In this way, you will renounce something so that someone else can receive what you have renounced. He will satisfy his hunger and pray for you and your sacrifice will be pleasing to God.

Didacus (3rd Century):

If someone is poor, he should fast and give to his brothers what he would have spent on fast days.

Saint Augustine (354-430):

Will your fasting be pleasing to God if you forget your brother? To fast and to share: prayer receives its flight carried by two wings. You are to fast in such a way so that someone else can eat instead of you, and you are to rejoice for being able to give your meal. The One who has no food wants to be fed in the poor. Let us be on guard not to despise our God in the poor Who is hungry in them.

St. Peter Chrysologus (450):

Not only fasting, but all virtues are wiped away without mercy.

St. Leo the Great (461):

The prayer of fasting is pleasing to God and frightful to Satan. It contributes to the salvation of others as well as to our own. There is nothing more efficacious than fasting in order to come closer to God.

Let us not neglect this powerful means, this therapy so effectual for our wounds. Evaluate your happiness: those who have received much should give much. May the fast of the faithful become food for the poor.

St. Fulgentius of Ruspe (533):

When we satisfy the passion of pleasure for food, that enjoyment has consumed the part that had to be given to the poor.

Rathier Veron (974):
Those who do not share with the poor what they themselves have not eaten, fast poorly. They keep it for their own mouths or worse yet, for the mammon, the evil spirit of greed.

Ralph of Poitier (1190):

When we fast, at our table we receive Christ in the poor.[11]

7.4. A Conversation between a Master and a Disciple about Fasting

"My child, what do you do when you fast?"

The brother answered, "In the morning I weave palm branches and as I work, I reflect on the psalms. When I finish a basket, I pray and at noon, I sleep a little. When I rise, I go to my room and work again until I have woven three baskets. In the evening, I pray and after giving one hundred gifts, I pray the office. The next day, I cook until the ninth hour and eat until I am full."

The old man responded, "My child, this is not fasting. If you renounce food and say something bad about someone; if you judge; if you are vengeful towards someone; if you permit bad thoughts to enter in or if, in your spirit, you long to do something else – it would be much better for you to avoid this by spending the day eating, instead of filling yourself with it. What use is it for a man to renounce food and give in to all other lusts? Do you not know that everyone, who indulges in his desires and thoughts, eats and drinks even though he does not take food? Instead, if you want to live perseverance and fast in a way pleasing to God, protect yourself from every bad word, every gossip, every condemnation and do not open your ear to bad speech. Cleanse your heart from every corporeal and spiritual stain (cf. 2 Cor 7,1) from every desire for revenge, and from all envy." [12]

---

[11] Lejeune, René, *Jeûne, guérison and fête du corps et de l'esprit*, Parvis, Hauteville, 3rd Issue, 1991. p. 162-163.
[12] Grün, *Fasten*, p. 28.

VIII. A WEEK OF A LIFE WITH BREAD AND WATER

For quite some time, I have personally led weeklong retreats of a life with bread and water. From the very title, 'Life with Bread and Water,' it should be clear that the week is not fasting in a strict sense, as it is in various clinics where fasting is offered as a form of therapy. In such other fasts, it is a matter of absolute fasting which begins with a complete cleansing of the organism and ends with several days of returning to a normal consumption of food. Such complete fasts last between one and four weeks and their principal goal is physical and psychological, although the spiritual dimension is not excluded. There is a large list of illnesses that are being treated by means of such fasts. They are especially offered to individuals with heart problems. In such therapeutic fasting, a doctor who monitors the individuals is always present.[13]

Our week of a 'life with bread' begins after the evening program at St. James' Church. This is not a complete fast, but one where bread is taken. For this reason, a complete cleansing of the organism is not necessary as it is with therapeutic fasting where special additives are taken with water.

For first-time participants in a week of 'living with bread' it is always explained how, when and how much bread is to be eaten and how much water is to be taken. This is very important.

---

[13] Cf. BUCHINGER, Otto, dr. med. i BUCHINGER, Andreas, *Das heilende Fasten,* Dr. Werner Jopp Verlag, Wiesbaden, 1991., 4th printing.
BUCHINGER, Otto jun., *Das Heilfasten und seine Hilfsmethoden als biologischer Weg*, Hypokrates Verlag, Stuttgart, 1992., 22nd printing.
FAHRNER, Heinz, *Fasten als Therapie, Physiologie und Pathophysiologie, Methodik, Indikationen und Verläufe, Psychologische Aspekte*, Hypokrates Verlag, Stuttagrt, 1991.
FRIEBEL, Gisela, *Gesundheit fast zum Nulltarif,* Vier Flamingos Verlag, Rheine, 1991.

8.1. Drinking Bread and Eating Water

This is an actual title: bread needs to be drunk and water, eaten! Even if at first glance this may seem strange, this is the way it is. This means that the bread needs to be chewed until it becomes liquid. In therapeutic fasting, this was first offered for heart patients by Dr. Mayr of Austria; it is said that bread needs to be chewed 60 times before a sip of milk is taken. Then it is chewed again another 30 times.

Everyone who has gone to school knows that two-thirds of food digestion should take place in the mouth where direct preparation for further digestion takes place. Whoever does this eases the digestion process for his organism. In this way, much energy the organism would otherwise need to use if the food is not chewed well is saved. It is also clear that the first part of digestion in the mouth cannot take place if one eats a lot and quickly. In doing so, there is no real preparation of the food. This results in many problems for the organism: it starts to lose balance; because of being overworked, it is more prone to sickness and it loses much nutritional value.

While eating slowly in this manner, no liquid should be taken so that the glands secreting the necessary enzymes for the digestive process in the mouth and in the rest of the organism are activated.

When the organism sends the first signal that it has had enough, one stops taking bread and begins to take liquids. It is necessary to drink slowly and enough.

With this fast, a person does not renounce food for a period of time but reduces it to a minimum.

It is said that a person who claims to eat normally actually consumes a third more than he needs. This can easily happen when someone eats quickly because he cannot know how much his organism needs. In this way, the contact is lost between the organism that sends signals when it has had enough and the conscious response from the brain. This is injurious for every organism.

During these retreats, water and tea are offered and a minimum of 3 quarts of liquid is recommended daily. Bread is eaten three times a day: for breakfast, lunch and dinner, while water or tea are recommended between meals as well.

8.2. A Therapeutic Description of Fasting According to Dr. Mayr

After what has been said, it would be beneficial to look at what is done in a therapeutic fast according to Dr. Mayr. The following description and personal experience of a woman doctor can help us Christians more easily decide to fast in the Biblical and spiritual sense – as confirmed by Church tradition and practice.

"As a doctor, for years, I have been accompanying patients in a therapeutic method of fasting developed by Dr. F.X. Mayr. I have personally experienced a healing from migraine headaches through fasting, although not every migraine can be healed in this way.

With the therapeutic fasting according to Dr. Franz-Xavier Mayr, protection, education and purification are essential. Protection pertains to the body. Excessive physical strain should be avoided. It is good to walk several hours a day and to rest at least half an hour before lunch and to go to bed around 9 p.m. in the evening. Generally speaking, it is never good to eat when one is tired. That is why it is better to rest in bed before a meal. When we are tired, the digestion in the stomach is very strained.

The protection that pertains to the mind consists of not thinking of problems while fasting, as far as this is possible. For example, practically speaking it would not be advisable to visit a couple in a marital crisis on fast days. While fasting, one becomes sensitive. In the first days, a part of the person becomes depressive and another part, aggressive. This is good to know since difficult dreams could be experienced.

As for education, we must all learn how to eat and consume food. Especially the chewing of food is taught. Every bite needs to be chewed 60 times. Such conscious chewing should be a lifelong practice.

Purification pertains to the emptying of the intestines with bitter salt. The physical cleansing by fasting can be compared to a summer cleaning of an old stove of all the sediments accumulated over time."

"During fasting, the body is freed from all deposits and excesses. There is a cleansing of the organism from various acids that also affect the psychological level – people become 'sour'. In the first days of fasting when the body is being freed from poisons, there is a stronger elimination of liquids. Because of this process, even a face, which appeared gloomy and dark, can become more clear and beautiful.

During the life of Dr. Mayr people could even fast even for six weeks without any problems or danger. Today, this is often not possible because a fundamental component is generally present even at nighttime. A person tends to wake up at 2 a.m. -- which is the 'time of the liver'. The liver has an assignment of eliminating all the stomach waste so as to liberate the organism of poisons. That is why it is good to put a warm damp cloth on the upper part of the body (a damp cloth with a hot water bottle on top) prior to the noon rest and before going to sleep.

Possibly, certain minerals need to be added. The goal of therapeutic fasting of Dr. Mayr is under no circumstance for losing weight, but for cleansing and enhancing the physical health and for healing of many illnesses. Special success has been noted with stomach problems, digestive tract problems (syndrome of enteropathy), senior diabetes, high blood pressure, various skin diseases and other illnesses."

Program outline:

On an empty stomach, a glass of warm water with one teaspoon of diluted bitter salt is taken in the morning. This is followed by as much physical movement as possible. After the drink of bitter salt or before breakfast, one must first shower with warm water and then with cold. Then the body must be well massaged to increase blood circulation. Due to the process of elimination of toxins through the lungs, it is possible to experience bad breath.

It is possible to eat breakfast after half an hour of taking the bitter salt. For breakfast and lunch, one or more pieces of day-old bread (not fresh) is/are taken with one cup of milk. Dr. Mayr started this way. Because today there are an increasing number of people allergic to wheat and milk, wheat bread can be substituted with rye or rice bread. It is important to know that solid food is necessary only as an aid for chewing. Milk can be substituted with tea, warm water, whole milk, etc. After the first two days, it is good to decide for one type of solid and one type of liquid food because uniformity is of a great help.

While eating, every bite should be chewed at least 60 times. Then a tablespoon of liquid should be taken and the same bite chewed another 20 to 30 times. This chewing helps to increase secretion of saliva, beginning digestion. Poor food intake unfortunately starts in infancy. When a nursing child does not sufficiently engage in the act of 'nursing' to get the mother's milk, he is made a 'drunkard' in being given a bottle of milk with a large opening.

One should eat in this way until there is a first notion of fullness, then immediately stop eating and drinking. According To Dr. Mayr, at least 5 hours should lapse between meals. For supper, a cup of tea is taken with a tablespoon of honey, if necessary. Tea is consumed a spoonful at a time which aids in the feeling of being full. If someone is really hungry, some bread can be eaten and chewed in the manner described. Generally speaking, it is very important to drink liquids if one feels hunger or if other difficulties arise. In such situations, other necessary ingredients can be included or increased for cleansing the stomach.

While fasting, and in general, it is very important to drink at least 1.36 ounces of liquid for each 2.2 pounds of body weight. For example, if a person weighs 110 pounds they should drink at least 2 quarts of liquid. Water or tea is suggested. Acidic teas such as hibiscus should not be taken nor should chamomile which leads to excessive relaxation of the intestines. Black tea and coffee should always be avoided. Liquid can be consumed 15 minutes before meals. If the liquid is cold, it should be consumed half an hour before the meal because it must first be warmed inside the stomach before leaving it. No liquids should be taken until 45 minutes after the meal. It is recommended that two-thirds of the liquid be consumed in the first half of the day so as not to disturb the night's rest. (cf. - Rauch: Die Darmreinigung nach F.X. Mayr i Blut–und Säftereinigung)

The duration of this therapeutic fast could be up to three weeks. In order to return to a normal consumption of food, another three weeks are necessary during which the intake of bitter salt is slowly reduced. (cf. - Rauch: Milde Ableitungsdiät)

During this time, as always, it is very important to watch for a proper balance of necessary food ingredients. Majority of people are taxed by acidity which causes many illnesses. The most important 'producers' of acidity are coffee, sugar, meat and insufficient exercise.

According to Dr. Mayr, the therapeutic fast can help in the consumption and choice of food after the fast. The more frequently one fasts, (doctors generally recommend three weeks a year) the more aware one becomes of their physical wants. Patients have often said to me, "I made a mistake again" because they did something wrong – either they ate too much or at the *wrong time. This is certainly not a sin, but in any case, it is foolishness or a lack of care.*

Interior preparation for the consumption of food is equally as important as the food. Before eating, one needs to give thanks and eat joyfully. Individuals who have experienced a great psychological burden such as a death, a fear of dying from hunger or a psychosis, should not fast. People who need medication must find a doctor who is familiar with the therapeutic fast of Dr. Mayr to monitor them during their fast. Three times a week a doctor carries out a 'stomach treatment'. This includes gentle toning of the large and small intestine, alleviation of the liver and breathing therapy. During the doctor's appointment, it is also possible to address other problems.

As a first reaction to therapeutic fasting, it is possible for all illnesses and life's disorders especially headaches, depression and aggression, to appear. To ease these kinds of reactions a week of 'preparation for fasting' is recommended. During this time, bitter salt starts to be taken and sugar, even where it is indirectly found such as in canned foods, tomato sauce, etc., is eliminated. Nothing uncooked is consumed. Coffee and black tea are also eliminated and supper is substituted for tea with honey and some old bread, if necessary.

A consultation with a doctor is very important before starting the therapeutic fast, in order for it to be adapted to various conditions such as of being overweight or anemic or for athletes. In Dr. Mayr's framework of therapeutic fasting, there is also a fasting with a tea for weight lost. Also, with the cleansing and healing of the intestines, those who are underweight can start to gain weight.

A woman who has experienced Dr. Mayr's method of fasting and has led others in it, participated in a fasting and prayer seminar. In Medjugorje in October of 1999, she stated:

"My experience with Dr. Mayr's therapeutic fasting was a good foundation for fasting on bread and water. So far as 'protection' is concerned, I understood that it was necessary to 'pull away' from all external obligations; to leave every worldly concern and difficulty and to abandon everything that could be a burden.

So far as 'education' is concerned, I understood how it is possible to attain silence when eating slowly. I received a treasured experience of being able to pray the prayer of Jesus at mealtime so as to be able to pronounce His Holy Name with every bite.

During this fast, a new dimension was opened for me as I came to realize that fasting is, first of all, a 'preparation' for the Eucharist, which is always connected with fasting. A sentence I heard at a lecture became deeply sealed in my heart: 'A person of the Eucharist can have no other way but the way of bread.' At the same time, fasting is a 'preparation' for the great feast to which the Kingdom of God is compared, and which comes at the end.

While fasting, I became aware that I was more open. That is why, temptations also came but were more easily recognizable and then overcome, as the Pope tells us in his encyclical, 'The Gospel of Life'. I myself have not experienced this dimension of fasting. Namely, I had not felt a greater temptation. Instead, I experienced, especially during night Adoration, something I had not known before – a state of 'being awake', a spiritual openness and giving. I am very grateful for this experience. From the lectures I understood that we are only able to create the conditions for experiencing God's love; just like for the growth of seed conditions for growth, can be created. The actual growth is something else. In Medjugorje, Mary has clearly conveyed the conditions in Her messages: FAST AND PRAY.

When my reason again asks me, 'Why fasting in particular?' I can console myself by saying that I don't have to understand everything at any price. A little child does not need to understand everything, and next to

Mary, I am a little child. For me it is enough to know that by fasting, I prepare joy for Her. In Her message of September 25ᵗʰ, 1985, She said, '. . . and you will prepare a joy from me by this.' " [14]

8.3. A Full Stomach does not Pray Willingly

An Old Latin proverb speaks about a generally accepted human experience: *Plenus venter non-studet libenter –* '*a full stomach does not learn willingly.*' When the stomach is full, it is not possible to learn. For digestion to take place, the stomach must draw as much blood as possible from the organism. When the blood is thus drawn from the brain, a person feels tired and has to rest. The same rule applies to prayer: *a full stomach does not pray willingly*. It must rest and sleep. Therefore, it is understandable why a person is much fresher while fasting. After a brief period of tiredness and the need to sleep because of the metabolism, there is freshness and the need for sleep is reduced. This increases the work ability.

In Canada this expression was slightly changed although its meaning is the same: '*A full stomach has no ears.*' General experience, especially today, reveals the truth of this expression. A person who is full becomes incapable of listening. Occupied with himself, he is deaf to others. This is how it is possible to understand all the problems in the family and in school education: the children are full, actually too full, and do not have enough strength to hear others. This also endangers the listening to God's Word. Someone, who does not hear the Word, cannot respond to it.

From what has been said, one must never conclude that it is better for a person to go hungry and have as little as possible. There is a need here to be mindful of the fact that, more than ever, fasting is necessary for today's man. By fasting and prayer, a person more

---

[14] This woman wants to remain anonymous although she gladly shared her experience at the fasting and prayer seminar and of the therapeutic fast of Dr. Mayr. She belongs to an Evangelical community.

easily opens himself to God and to others. He hears others more easily, understands them better and answers more efficaciously to the words directed to him.

Looked at from this standpoint, Mary's message to fast two days a week becomes even more concrete. When the all-encompassing value of fasting is understood, it is easier to decide to fast. While the truth that man is not an angel remains, namely, that he has a spirit, a soul and a body; the fact also remains that he cannot live perfectly in this world. This perfection awaits us in the Eternal Kingdom of God. Until then, nothing else is left to us but to fight for the inner freedom day by day so as always to be prepared to listen to, and to accept, the words directed to us by God and others.

8.4. Balanced Weight

God created the human organism to be very wise. It is difficult to answer the question of what happened to balanced weight. However, a supposition can be made about how this balance was destroyed or distorted.

Already at a young age, every child, even one on mother's milk, stops eating at a given moment. Once satiated, its organism sends signals to the brain which then sends a 'command' to stop eating; and the child does so. If the child starts crying because it seeks the nearness of its mother or father, it can easily happen that the child is given more food instead. This especially happens when the mother or father does not have the time to be with the child. It is an easier solution to feed the child again or to give him a 'pacifier' that actually deceives his organism. These are the first blows to weight balance. Afterwards, this is continually repeated when the child is forced to eat more; and especially when he is told that it is a shame to leave what has been prepared. This has happened to all of us many times both at home and at our friends' house. In such circumstances, the true connection between the organism and the control center in the brain is lost and a way for disorder in the organism is opened. Over time, this becomes a regular occurrence.

Additionally, it is our experience that we often eat not because we are hungry but because we are nervous. A person who is nervous more easily reaches for an excess of alcohol or for intoxicating drugs. In the same way, it is possible to eat excessively due to stress and nervousness. Generally, by doing so, great problems for the heart and the blood system are being prepared.

I recall meeting a woman who weighted 60 more pounds than she should have. She decided to go on a diet and, under doctors' care, started to 'take off' the pounds. In conversation, her friend explained how this is normal. She said that this lady had a very responsible job with great stress so she ate more at home. I reacted and reprimanded her friend saying, "If you are her real friend, after a stressful situation go for a walk in the park with her or go for a swim with her and then eat normally!"

Every pound that exceeds the ideal weight becomes a real burden for the organism and creates a need for more food because the added excess wants to be maintained. In this way, a vicious cycle takes place which, in the end, leads to other disturbances in the organism. The organism becomes more prone to illnesses since the defense mechanism weakens and becomes more easily damaged. All therapeutic effects of fasting can be understood from this standpoint. An organism must be helped to return to its ideal weight in order to be able again to return to health and freshness; to be protected from every fatigue and to rest more easily.

IX. FASTING AND PRAYER AND MENTAL HEALTH

An old proverb says, *"A healthy mind - in a healthy body"*, but it can also be said, *"a healthy body through a healthy mind!"* Man, in himself is a unique wholeness although it is possible to speak about his body, mind and soul. The state of one is maintained by, and influences, the state of the others.

It is clear that fasting has a positive influence on the health of the body and on the maintenance of balance. In that, directly or indirectly, it has a positive influence on the state of the mind, the psyche. When the physical balance is lost, mental stability is also threatened and lost balance on a mental level is expressed on the physical level. Perhaps this can best be seen in two extreme states of the mind that are reflected in the body: bulimia and anorexia. Bulimia is the excess consumption of food followed by self-induced vomiting while anorexia is the rejection of food. Both situations exhibit a mental illness that come about as a result of wounded interpersonal relationships and in wounded relationships with oneself and nature.

Healing begins when the mind becomes free of negative and strained relationships with oneself and with others. On this level, fasting and prayer are actually a form of mental hygiene. The basis of mental illness is a loss of inner freedom. When a person imprisons himself by material things and by pleasures, he actually becomes a slave to himself, to others and to material things. In such a state, he is on the way to self-destruction. How many individuals have destroyed their physical and mental health because they were wounded and overburdened? They sought peace and solutions to their problems in alcohol, drugs and other addictions. It is a known fact that there is an increasing number of addicts and those suffering from depression who have lost the meaning of life. There are more and more people becoming addicted to medication in which they seek tranquility. All of this reflects on the physical state of the person.

It is not my intention to enter into all of the psycho-pathological problems or to offer a simplified solution for all mental illness; nor is it to give false hope to those who carry the cross of mental illness. I only desire to draw attention to the fact that, through fasting and prayer, the mind more easily retains its health and its peace.

That is why it is important to understand that we need to protect ourselves from every form of slavery, that is, to nurture inner freedom. This begins from early childhood. When we ask ourselves if children should fast, the answer is affirmative. Clearly, it is not a matter of a fast that an adult needs to do, but of a correct education for a proper relationship with oneself and others.

When children live in over-abundance from the beginning, receiving everything they want immediately and without effort, some of their developmental stages do not form properly and deficiencies are experienced later in life. When there are only one or two children in a family, they grow up in an environment in which they become egocentric and fail to develop adequate personal relationships with others. However, life is not easy. It brings problems and difficulties and demands a battle in which one wins or loses. In this battle, one does not always get what is wanted immediately or without personal effort. The entire mental make-up of someone who is used to receiving everything without any personal effort in his childhood - of someone who looks at others only inasmuch as they can be of use to him - collapses and fails. This is why there are increasing numbers of unstable individuals who lose the meaning of life the moment they experience their first failure in school, at work or in love. They have no joy in life and, compelled by selfishness, they go the way of continual destruction of themselves and of others. It is here that depression and violence are born in their various forms.

Everything I want to say can be simply expressed in the following image. If someone wants to observe a painting to enjoy its beauty, he has to step away or step back in order to see all of its details. If a person is too close to the artwork, he will concentrate on individual aspects, which only gain their meaning in context of the whole picture. For this reason, it is possible for someone to notice only a shadow, or a dark point, or a crooked line; or even just a flower or a pretty color. In neither situation is the observer able to evaluate the painting. While one is in danger of proclaiming that the painting is dark and the other that it is completely light, neither evaluation is correct. Both the shadow and the light have their respective roles. It is the same with a person who has lost inner freedom. He is too close to himself, to material things and to others. Because, from his perspective, he loses the 'wholeness' of life, he creates unhealthy relationships.

It is good for every person, especially for a child, to have enough to live on. However, from an early age, it is important to learn to look at life and everything in life with a freedom of heart and soul. This can be attained if the family fasts for two days a week as Our Lady is asking. It is necessary to explain to the children that on those two days, nothing that is in any way excessive or unnecessary is to be taken. For example, if someone gives a child a chocolate on a Wednesday or a Friday, the child is told that although the chocolate is his, to leave it for tomorrow. The period of time until then becomes a time of spiritual training. In this way, the child practices looking at what he loves and wants and he leaves it for the future. The child thus learns not to grab at things with greed and selfishness. In this way, an inner freedom is realized helping the child to develop later a positive relationship with himself, with others and with material things.

9.1. Entering Within and Becoming Silent

During the entire fasting and prayer seminar, silence is advised. The reasons are simple. Every person receives daily a myriad of news items from around the world by today's means of communication through newspapers, radio, television and other media. Faced with these means of communication, a person remains a mute observer, reader or listener; someone who receives news about everything that is happening. At the same time, he easily forgets everything and daily seeks more news in order to reiterate the information to his friends; to those who have heard, read and seen the same thing. In this way, language skills and the general power of expression are impoverished.

On the other hand, we continually hear that it is not possible to believe anyone; how no one lives up to his or her word and how people are superficial. Often it is said that diplomats do not say what they are thinking and do not do what they are saying. This is actually a disgrace to the gift of words and speech.

It is well known that deafening music is generally played where youth gather at various celebrations. It is also known that in most nightclubs and discos people sit, drink and dance with loud music for the entire night. This points to an inner emptiness that seeks to be filled. The greater our emptiness is, the greater the need for noise and shouting. It is in this emptiness that violence and violent words are born. On this basis, a conclusion is reached that man is incapable of silence and stillness; and yet where there is no stillness and silence, proper words cannot be conceived or born. For this reason, there are less good and noble words being spoken and all the more empty, violent, offensive and inappropriate ones.

Often seminar participants admitted to me that it was more difficult for them to be silent than to live with bread. Particularly because of this, the call to silence and stillness becomes even more significant. It is not a matter of speech being forbidden or the gift of speech being renounced. Instead, it is a matter of enabling people to speak.

Stillness and silence are entered into with two questions in mind, 'Where is my word conceived?' and 'How is it born?' If a word is conceived in anger, resentment, hatred, jealousy, envy, sorrow, depression, addiction, selfishness, pride or in some other negative environment, then it is a word that insults, humiliates, brings lack of peace and discomfort and offends the hearts of others. The moment that the person calms down, he often says, "I did not mean that, forgive me…" or something similar. A person does not stand behind a word that is conceived and born in such a way. He apologizes for it. However, if a word is conceived in peace, love, trust, hope, joy, friendship and goodness, it brings among men that in which it was conceived. It is born as a word that builds and a person does not apologize for it. Such words remain.

We must not forget what is said at the beginning of St. John's Gospel, "in the beginning was the Word, and the Word was with God and the Word was God." (Jn 1,1) Jesus Himself tells us that He is the Word of the Father. What the Father says is His Word and the Father stands behind His Word. This is why He can say that the Father and He are one. He never has to withdraw His word. It remains forever. It is eternal.

Jesus told us to let our 'yes' mean 'yes' and our 'no' mean 'no'. (cf. Mt 5,37) Clearly it is not a matter of speech being forbidden or reduced to two words. It means always to be aware of what is being said and to stand behind what was said.

In the same way, it can be said that man is his word and that his word is man inasmuch as that word is born in peace, love, friendship and trust. That is why it is so important to remain in stillness and silence from time to time in order to re-examine our relationship with our word, because we are our word and our word is who we are. The calmer the person is and the more he is present in himself, the simpler, calmer and more beautiful his word is. The word is not only an expression of man, but is man himself. However, the more broken and dependent a person is, the more his word will also be. It is good to note that in the Church, many acts of devotion such as vows (a deliberate and free promise to God), ordination and others, consist of very few words or only of the 'laying on of hands'.

The power must be returned to the word. The word does not receive its power by tumult or shouting, but by the level of the soul where it is born.

Today, we often hear that the authority of parents and educators is threatened and, in that, education is also threatened. In anger, a parent or a teacher may ask his child or student to do something or forbid him to do something. Afterwards, rightly so, the parent or teacher seeing that this was not good, changes his mind or his demands. He then softens the restriction or removes it altogether. By doing this, he deeply shakes his authority and wounds the child. In turn, the child does not discover real values or the meaning of being forbidden to do something in his education. Instead, he connects everything to the disposition of the authority. For him, what is good or bad depends on the authority. In this way, the real sense of value is lost and a spiritual emptiness takes place.

It is not accidental that so many people today have lost a real relationship with themselves, with others, with nature and with God. The more that the word loses in value, the more shaken are the values generally.

In the following text, we can come to understand what St. James says about the tongue and the word:

"Not many of you should become teachers, my brothers, for you realize that we will be judged more strictly, for we all fall short in many respects. If anyone does not fall short in speech, he is a perfect man, able to bridle his whole body also. If we put bits into the mouths of horses to make them obey us, we also guide their whole

bodies. It is the same with ships: even though they are so large and driven by fierce winds, they are steered by a very small rudder wherever the pilot's inclination wishes. In the same way the tongue is a small member and yet has great pretensions.

Consider how small a fire can set a huge forest ablaze. The tongue is also a fire. It exists among our members as a world of malice, defiling the whole body and setting the entire course of our lives on fire, itself set on fire by Gehenna. For every kind of beast and bird, of reptile and sea creature, can be tamed and has been tamed by the human species, but no human being can tame the tongue. It is a restful evil, full of deadly poison.

With it we bless the Lord and Father, and with it we curse human beings who are made in the likeness of God. From the same mouth come blessing and cursing. Does a spring gush forth from the same opening both pure and brackish water? Can a fig tree, my brothers, produce olives, or a grapevine, figs? Neither can salt water yield fresh." (Jas 3,1-12)

What is first necessary is to decide for silence; to say nothing other than what is essential. This is one of the conditions for man to enter into himself and to create conditions for interior processes through fasting and prayer. Even though it is difficult to be silent, as the seminar experience confirms, it is even more difficult to enter into interior silence – to silence the imagination, memory and feelings – and to create a new space for meeting with God. Only when interior silence is realized can it be said that a part of purification has taken place and that a new relationship with self, others and God can begin.

9.2. Texts about Silence

"STAND STILL!, my soul, for so thy Lord commands:
E'en when thy way seems blocked,
leave it in His wise hands;
His arm is mighty to divide the wave.

STAND STILL!, my soul, STAND STILL! –
and thou shalt see how God can work the impossible for
thee, for with a great deliverance He doth save!
"Be not impatient, but in stillness stand,
even when compassed 'round on every hand,
in ways thy spirit does not comprehend.
God cannot clear thy way till thou art still,
that He may work in thee His blessed will,
and all thy heart and will to Him do bend.

"BE STILL!, my soul, for just as thou art still,
can God reveal Himself to thee;
until through thee His love and light and life can freely
flow; in stillness God can work through thee and reach
the souls around thee.
He then through thee can teach His lessons,
and His power in weakness show!

"BE STILL! -- a deeper step in faith and rest.
"Be still and know!" thy Father knoweth best the way to
lead His child to that fair land, a "Summer" land, where
quiet waters flow;
where longing souls are satisfied, and "know their God",
and praise for all that He has planned!"

Anonymous

"God is the friend of silence. Trees, flowers, grass grow
in silence. See the stars, moon, and sun how they move
in silence."

Mother Teresa of Calcutta

It is everything, it is perfection, it is salvation. To close
the physical eyes, to open the eyes of the heart and to
be immersed in Your presence.

I will gather myself and my distractions, and will entrust
myself to You. I place myself into You as into a great
hand.

It is not necessary for me to speak in order for You to
hear me. I do not need to enumerate what I don't have,

nor do I need to tell You what is happening in this world or why we need Your help.

I don't want to run away from people or to evade them. Nor will I hate noise and haste. I only want to include them in my silence and to be prepared for You.

I want to be silent in the place of all those who rush, make noise and are distressed; I want to have time in place of all those who have no time.

With my senses and thoughts, I wait for You to come.

Lord, to be in You is all I ask for myself. In that, I receive everything I need for time and eternity. The more devout and sincere my prayer is, the less I have to say. In the end – I have become completely silent. And I have become – a listener. And that is something completely opposite of speaking.

Sören Kierkegaard

Prayers before Meditation

Lord, prepare my heart, my spirit, my senses, and my soul for You.

Create silence in me and when everything is completely still, fill my silent emptiness with Your presence Lord; with Your gentle light, Your wisdom and love.

With every breath I breathe, awaken in me the sense of Your presence until it becomes knowledge and conviction for me.

Grant me rest in Your silence without images and imagination.

And when my time draws near Lord, grant that I may hear the message, the word - which will bear fruit in me in due time.

Otto Gillen

Sit still in the solitude of your room. Bow your head, close your eyes, breathe silently and slowly, gather your thoughts and your reason. Still your heart and in the rhythm of your breath pronounce the words: "Lord Jesus Christ, Son of God, have mercy on me." Pronounce these words softly and simply; cast out all other thoughts. Persevere and be patient. Repeat this exercise often.

Admission of a Russian Pilgrim

If man prepares peace within himself through silence so that every noise disappears, the Lord comes in a soft breeze as He did to Elija and illuminates the spirit.

John Tauler

Interior prayer is silence, 'a sign of the world to come' (St. Isaac Ninevite) or 'silent love'.

St. John of the Cross

A method of the way towards God is to remove everything that hinders. It is to remove everything blaring and impure; to remove everything worldly. But when we have removed everything worldly from our souls what is left to us who are worldly? Silence. Darkness. And in that darkness: God.

Dionysius of Areopagite

The closer we are to God, the more miserly our words become. When we use many words instead of Adoring, instead of honoring, instead of falling to our knees with reverential fear, we still remain far from God. The closer we are to God, the quieter it becomes - and silence begins. Then even questions stop. Then we are with God.[15]

Dionysius of Areopagite

---

[15] Herceg, Fr. Mladen, *Jeka Tišine*, Zagreb, 1998., For private use, pp. 64,68, 74, 78, 80, 84.

X. FASTING AND SPIRITUAL HEALTH

Having reflected on fasting in relation to physical and mental health, it remains for us to reflect on spiritual fruits of fasting and prayer.

The goal of a Christian life is to become similar to Christ - to become completely like Him. We are called to accept and to try to live in a way that helps us truly realize this. Fasting and prayer, in themselves, do not have meaning. Their importance is only in relation to reaching a goal; and a Christian who wants to become similar to Christ must have absolutely concrete goals that he must accomplish. When we speak about spiritual health, we must emphasize that it also has a positive effect on the mental and physical health. This does not mean that a physical illness is proof of a lack of mental or spiritual health. We are familiar with saints who had physical illnesses during their entire lives, but through their illness, they achieved perfect spiritual health.

There are also sure measures for spiritual health. These are interior freedom and peace, an ability to love and to forgive, generosity and gratitude, complete surrender to the Will of God and readiness to sacrifice one's life for others. In other words, the goal of a Christian life is to be able to say to God and to those we live with: "This is my life for you, my gifts are at your service."

10.1. God in the First Place

God made man's heart for Himself and it cannot be happy if God is not in the first place. It is sufficient for each person to ask himself what influences his concrete decisions in order to know what place God has in his life. When God becomes the measure of all decisions and of every action, then it is possible to speak about God being in the first place.

This is what it was like in Jesus' life. Everything He did was according to the Will of the Father and He did only His Father's Will. He is completely in the Father as the Father is in Him. The words He spoke He did not speak of Himself but were those He heard from the Father. While fasting in the desert, when He had to fight against the tempter, He did everything in order for the Father to be glorified and Adored and for His Word to be life for all. He did not permit the Father to be put to the test. When He was experiencing the deathly battle in the Garden of Gethsemane, He again completely surrendered Himself to the Will of the Father. On the Cross, He commended His Spirit into the Father's hands. The first place in man's heart, at every moment of his life, belongs to God.

If a person remains only on the level of prayer, selfishness and pride can easily sneak into the spirit of prayer and prayer intentions. Even though we say, "Father, Your Will be done," we, none the less, expect things to be as we want them to be. This is why it can easily happen that a person who prays measures God's love, mercy and goodness according to what he has received or did not receive, in relation to what he prayed for. In this way, it is possible for an entire life of prayer to remain only a battle between man's will and God's Will.

It is not an exaggeration to say that our prayer can even be Godless, namely, that we do not seek God, His Will, His love, nor His Kingdom in it. Instead, we seek Him inasmuch as He can give us something. This is why Jesus warns us to seek first the Kingdom of God and His justice and the rest will be added onto us. (cf. Mt 6,26-34) If we do not listen to Jesus, our prayer will be inspired by our needs. If God does not give us what we are asking for, we will then turn away from Him disappointed because He did not give us what we wanted.

However, whoever accepts the call and starts to pray and live with bread (practically speaking for the two days of a life with bread this means to leave everything else except for bread), he enters into a process of freeing his heart from selfishness and pride. This process frees us from our attachment to our desires and wants as well as from our unhealthy addictions to material things. It frees us from an unhealthy attachment to ourselves and to others so that space becomes available for God to take the first place in our hearts. God does not occupy the heart in order to imprison it but to free it; to be its light, way, truth, life, peace and love – to be its everything.

Through fasting and prayer, a person becomes free and capable of living a life worthy of man. Everyone must bear in mind and must never forget that it is particularly this growth in freedom that is the measuring gauge for fasting and prayer. It is important always to be conscious of this, to examine oneself and not to be satisfied easily with the number of days fasted or the myriad of prayers pronounced. The life of Jesus and becoming like Him remain the main and only measurement. Fasting and prayer receive their meaning in the freeing of the heart. In this freedom that grows through fasting and prayer, a person becomes more sensitive to his relationship with himself, with others and with material things.

We are easily able to recognize if our fasting and prayer are spinning in a vicious circle of a lack of freedom. If this is so, fasting will only become an unpleasant renunciation from pleasant things and prayer will become a renunciation of our free time where we come to feel that praying is a waste of our time.

I am convinced that a person is not capable of renunciation but only of an exchange. Through fasting and prayer we discover 'what is better' so we can easily leave behind what is not good or is not as good. This is why we must never observe the life experience of saints and mystics from the standpoint of renunciation but of an exchange. It sounds unpleasant for us 'normal' Christians for someone to renounce their family, possessions and everything else, if we do not see that there has been an exchange for something better. It is particularly because of this that there are fewer and fewer Christians who are prepared to follow Christ radically. They do not see an exchange for what they are renouncing in the way Jesus Himself spoke of. (cf. Mk 10,28)

When renunciation is lived by a priest or a religious and 'a hundred-fold' is not received back as promised, the meaning of life, and work is sometimes lost. One remains bitter and agitated while life becomes empty, and then more and more real tragedies take place with those who are sent to proclaim the Good News.

For this reason, every Christian, especially a priest or a religious, must fast and pray. By practicing fasting and prayer, he enters into the mystery of God's Kingdom and His love. He becomes a person similar to Christ, capable of giving his life for others.

10.2. Awakening a Yearning for God

There are numerous prayers in both the Old and the New Testament in which deep longing is expressed for God, for peace, for joy, for light, for truth, for love and for everything that comes from God. It is sufficient to recall Psalm 63 in order to sense the essence of prayer and its actual first and fundamental condition. The Psalmist prays:

"O God, you are my God whom I seek; for you my flesh pines and my soul thirsts like the earth, parched, lifeless and without water. Thus have I gazed toward you in the sanctuary to see your power and your glory."

Whoever longs for God will have time for prayer; he will seek God and will find Him. Wherever this longing does not exist, there will be no prayer and no joyful anticipation of God or a meeting with Him. In Psalm 43, the Psalmist expresses his deep yearning for God in a very simple way. He compares his soul and heart with a hind that yearns for running waters:

"As the hind longs for the running waters, so my soul longs for you, O God. A thirst is my soul for God, the living God. When shall I go and behold the face of God? My tears are my food day and night, as they say to me day after day, 'Where is your God?' Those times I recall, now that I pour out my soul within me, when I went with the throng and led them in procession to the house of God, amid loud cries of joy and thanksgiving, with the multitude keeping festival."

A question is now posed: "How are we to bring to life this yearning which urges the soul to God as thirst urges the hind to the running water?" The answer is again found in fasting and prayer. The soul of the one who fasts and prays will be freer day by day, and in that freedom will seek God and will never cease seeking Him.

In the Beatitudes Jesus proclaims:

"Blessed are the poor in spirit, for theirs is the kingdom of heaven. . .Blessed are they who hunger and thirst for righteousness, for they will be satisfied. . . Blessed are the clean of heart, for they will see God. . ." (Mt 5,3;6;8)

The same problem is addressed. Those who are poor in spirit know that nothing can enrich them except for God. For this reason, they will seek Him and the Kingdom of Heaven will be theirs. Those who 'hunger and thirst' do not permit their yearning for what is of heaven to be replaced by a longing for the earthly bread and drink. They are of pure heart and know what is essential. They will not be blinded by anything of this world.

A yearning for God increases through fasting and prayer. This yearning is actually one of the criteria for the practice of our Christian fasting and prayer. Through it, the heart is being purified. It sees more clearly, opens itself more to spiritual values and does not permit itself to be stopped by anything in this world. At the same time, this is the dimension of fasting, which conducts the believer towards the heavenly feast and gives the eschatological meaning to fasting. It makes him capable of watching and waiting, of seeking and finding and then of beginning again without tiring. This, actually, is love. The essence of love consists in this: that the one who loves is always both near and far from the one he loves. He is always near because he loves. The physical distance of space is not a hindrance at all in that sense. The one who loves always feels far away and that is why the search for the beloved always starts anew.

In this way it is easy to understand the spiritual problems of today's man whose heart can easily turn to worldly desires and stop on the way toward God. This is the greatest deception that a person can experience. Through fasting and prayer this trap is exposed and easily overcome; so that, in this life's journey, man's heart and soul can always remain turned towards the One Whom he knows loves him immeasurably - God alone. This is the secret of all of the saints and mystics. They were tireless in their search for God and readily left everything to follow Him and to realize their yearning for Him. Their final realization was in eternity.

It is easy to see that where there is no fasting and prayer, the yearning for God is threatened and fasting and prayer again come into question. Mary calls us to fast and pray so that our hearts may always be free and may seek God without ceasing.

10.3. Fasting and Peace

Peace is a fruit of the Spirit.

The deepest longing of man's heart is actually for peace. In everything we do, whether good or bad, we seek peace. When a person loves, looks for and experiences peace or even when he hates and wants revenge, he seeks peace. When he stays sober or fights against addiction, he seeks peace. When he becomes drunk, he also seeks peace. When he fights for his life and the lives of those he loves, he realizes peace. Even when he raises his own hand against himself and commits suicide or kills someone, again he seeks peace. Therefore, every decision of man is, in its essence, a decision for peace.

Clearly when good is being done, personal peace and the peace of others are being realized. On the other hand, when evil is being committed, it is a search for one's own peace at the expense of the peace of others.

Looking at it from yet another perspective, we can see how often we lose peace because we are egotistical, selfish, envious, jealous, avaricious and consumed by power and honor. Experience confirms that through fasting and prayer, evil, egoism, and selfishness are overcome; the heart is opened and love and humility, generosity and goodness grow. Thus, true conditions for peace are realized. Whoever has peace because he loves and forgives also remains spiritually and physically healthy. He remains capable of shaping his own life in a manner worthy of man who is the most exalted of God's creatures. Through fasting and prayer, human needs are also diminished and brought to proportion. Also by this, conditions for peace along with a proper relationship with others and material things are being created.

This is why a misunderstanding comes about when fasting is experienced in a negative way as a renunciation of something; namely, when its benefit is not recognized on the spiritual level. For this reason, it is not possible to speak about replacing fasting with good works or anything else. In this context, we can understand why peace is always promised after conversion and after fasting and prayer.

Anselm Grün in his book on Fasting writes:

"In fasting, in particular, I become aware of, and am able to leave behind, the various means I use to try to replace my pleasures - which often stupefy or blind me - in order to recognize my deepest truth. Through fasting, I free myself of the encasement that has arched over my restless thoughts and feelings. In this way, everything that is within me can be revealed: my unfulfilled desires and longings, my passions, my thoughts which circle around me - around my success, my possessions, my health, my confirmations, and my feelings such as anger, bitterness and sorrow. The

wounds that I bury through numerous activities and by various means of self-consolation in food and drink are uncovered. Everything that is repressed comes to light. Fasting shows me who I am. It shows me where I am endangered and where I must start my battle."[16]

It is therefore, through fasting that a person comes to understand what he must fight against in himself. In this way, our subconscious is also freed from everything that drives us to restlessness and disorder. The soul then becomes still and conditions for peace are realized. The following text beautifully presents an image of this battle:

"When a king wants to occupy a city of the enemy he first seizes the water source and stops every supply. When the inhabitants begin to die from hunger and thirst, they surrender to him. This is what it is like with physical cravings: when a religious comes against them with fasting and hunger, the enemies of the soul lose strength." [17]

Experience clearly confirms that without a battle against internal enemies of peace, it is not possible to come to peace. This is why fasting is a very tried and tested means. This is also why it is not accidental that all of the prophets, together with Jesus and then the entire Church tradition, have called man to fasting and prayer so that he may open himself to true peace. The problem is that man is inclined to follow the way of false prophets who promise an easy peace that actual does not exist.

10.4. Fasting and Gratitude

Gratitude is an interior disposition of man who deeply and consciously experiences that he is God's creation. He realizes that he is not the master of his life and that life itself and everything he has have been given as a

---

[16] Grün, *Fasten*, pg. 23
[17] Miller, B. *Die Weisung der Väter*, Freiburg, 1965, p. 116

gift to him. It is in this disposition that yet another disposition is born - a responsibility before Him Who has entrusted everything to him. Whoever knows that whatever he has is a gift, will also know how to use these gifts in the service of others. He will be prepared to account for the gifts that he has received.

The joy of service, the joy for others to have the gifts and the ability to serve are included in gratitude. All of the gifts man receives are entrusted to him, but always for others. That is why our personal gifts have no meaning if they are not used to serve. It is just like the buried talent that the servant, out of fear, left un-used and in the end, returned to the master. He did not lose, defile or ruin the gift. He returned what he received and, in fact, this was his condemnation. (cf. Mt 24,14-30) It is clear from the above, that gratitude is a fruit of faith because faith teaches us that we ourselves are created and that everything we have is entrusted to us.

Humility also belongs to gratitude. Without humility, it is not possible to speak about a disposition of gratitude. The word for humility in German is *Demut*, which means a 'courage to serve.' The Latin expression *humilitas* comes from the root *humus* that means 'the best earth.' It indicates man's cooperation with God because man prepares his heart for the gifts to be able to grow and to be in service. Pride and selfishness are deadly spiritual viruses by means of which man begins to consider himself an independent master of what he has. He refuses to serve others and instead wants them to serve him. This is complete ingratitude.

When a person fasts and prays his heart is being freed from every slavery to himself and to his gifts but also from every slavery to others and to the world. Through fasting and prayer, a person frees himself from his own self and receives an interior space of freedom in which he can clearly see his truth and live it. In that freedom, a person recognizes everything that God does for him and does not forget it. In the same way, he recognizes everything that others do for him – all things big and small. *"Fasting helps man to again experience himself as the one who has received the gifts. Man sacrifices himself as a priority and creates a time and a place for God in prayer."* [18]

A grateful person is thus a person of peace who has joy and hope in his heart. He will never be disappointed because he never expects anything from others but does everything for them. However, when there is a disposition of ingratitude in the heart, there can be no peace or joy. Neither God nor man can ever sufficiently serve a selfish and egotistical person. He always seeks more from others, and when he does not receive it, he is disappointed. In that disappointment, violence, agitation and every other evil are born.

Every sin that takes place is actually a fruit of ingratitude. It is a fruit of selfishness and egoism. When a person does not see what God is doing for him and what others mean to him, he turns to himself and to the world. An ungrateful person is forgetful. This means that he forgets everything good only because of a single situation that does not appeal to him.

If we look at the original sin of Adam and Eve, we will be able to easily recognize forgetfulness and ingratitude. God created conditions for man to have a happy life. Man was forbidden only one thing – he was not to forget that he is a creature and that his Master exists. The tempter turned Eve's eyes away from everything she had and possessed and from everything she was permitted to touch and to enjoy. Instead he opened her eyes to what she did not have and what she was not permitted to do. The conversation between the tempter and Eve is a classic situation of how sin takes place. Eve's first reaction was good, 'The Lord said that we are not to touch this.' The tempter then asks the question found in every sin, 'Who is that God who forbids this to you?' Eve, forgetting everything that she had, reached

---

[18] Seeger, Hans-Karl, *Heilfasten – das Leben neu bedenken*, Butzon & Bercker, Kevelaer, 1998, p. 21.

her hand out for what she did not have – and sin took place. Had Eve said, 'First of all, I will touch everything that I am permitted to, and then I will do what I am forbidden', the tempter would never have been able to wait long enough for that moment of breach to take place because of so many things that were permitted. (cf. Gn 3,1-7)

When a person becomes blind to what others do for him (a wife, husband, parent, child, etc.,) and only sees what has not been done, he finds himself in a situation of forgetfulness and blindness and opens himself to sin. If we did not forget what our parents have done for us, there would never be a conflict between children and parents. If a husband did not forget what his wife has done for him, and vice versa, there would never be divorces. If we knew how to acknowledge each other and thank each other for what has been done for us, we would have joy and peace together.

Let us look at a family situation. When family members return home in the evening where the mother has worked all day, notice what she has done, and thank her for it, there is joy. However, if they first of all see what has not been done and start to complain and reprimand, a situation of arguments, attacks and defensiveness is born with consequent conflicts, lack of peace and sorrow.

Actually, the golden rule of every education is gratitude: to notice and to acknowledge what is good in the other person. A German saying states: "If the one who reprimands would rather praise, every reprimand could be endured."

A professional deformity is easily recognized here. We behave with each other as a teacher in school behaves when he first looks for mistakes and underlines them in red so that they are more clearly visible. Although this is not wrong, it is better to underline what is good so that the errors could be more easily endured. Whoever reacts only when someone makes a mistake loses every authority in the eyes of the one he reprimands. In many, negative reactions cause various insecurity complexes and bring about a conviction that life is valueless just because others fail to acknowledge the value of their work. Such dispositions can have a lifelong negative influence.

In order to develop a grateful relationship with God and others, we must decide to fast. Through fasting, a process of purification begins and continues. A pure heart and soul are grateful and are able to see both man and God better. They recognize and acknowledge others more easily.

When a person gains inner freedom, he becomes able to do good works and even to share his material goods with others. He is able to see clearly what he has and distinguish between what he needs and what he can give to others. This is why good works are expected from those who fast. Good works are a fruit of fasting and prayer and for this reason fasting and prayer cannot be replaced by them as is often inferred. When the prophet speaks about fasting that is not pleasing to God, he points out selfish behavior toward others. Isaiah says:

"This, rather, is the fasting I wish, releasing those bound unjustly, untying the thongs of the yoke; setting free the oppressed, breaking every yoke. Sharing your bread with the hungry, sheltering the oppressed and the homeless; clothing the naked when you see them, and not turning your back on your own." (Is 58,6,7)

With gratitude it is not so much a matter of saying the word, *'thank you'* as it is a matter of the most correct disposition a person must have toward himself as a creature, toward his gifts, toward God as the Benefactor of everything, toward others and toward material things.

When we look at Jesus' attitude of gratitude, we see that his entire life is a thanksgiving to the Father.

"At the Last Supper and the Cross, Jesus reveals the incentive of His entire life and of His death: thanksgiving

from His Heart. The Passion and Death of Jesus are necessary in order to fully glorify the Father (cf. Jn 17,1), but His entire life is a thanksgiving which is occasionally explicit and solemn so as to draw others to believe and to thank God with Him." [19] *(cf. Jn 11,42)*

This is the reason why a grateful person becomes a person of prayer. It is in this sense that the call to continual gratitude and prayer without ceasing can be understood. For St. Paul, a Christian life is a thanksgiving. (cf. Rom 1,8; 1 Thes 3,9 etc.)

A disposition of gratitude on earth passes over into eternal gratitude in Heaven. I will never forget the witness of one of the visionaries pertaining to this question. When she witnessed that Our Lady showed her Heaven, the visionary was asked: "What does one do in Heaven?" She answered, "In Heaven we give thanks and we will need all eternity for this thanksgiving when we realize all that God has done for us."

10.5. Fasting and Prayer

Fasting, prayer and good works are often mentioned together both by Jews and Christians. Prayer does not stand ahead of fasting and good works as independent of them, but as something that binds them from within. The most complete understanding of prayer is particularly offered in its connection with fasting. When we briefly look at what is said about prayer and how it is defined, we can see that the emphasis is naturally more on the state of the heart and soul and less on the body as a possible expression of prayer or of prayer generally.

The answer to the question, 'What is prayer?' is found in the Catechism of the Catholic Church. It is the definition of St. Thérèse of the Child Jesus: *"For me, prayer is a surge of the heart; it is a simple look turned toward heaven, it is a cry of recognition and of love, embracing both trial and joy."* It is also the definition of St. John

---

[19] Léon-Dufour, Xavier, *Dictionary of Biblical Theology*, Zagreb, 1993., IV Printing, p. 1482.

Damascene: *"Prayer is the raising of one's mind and heart to God or the requisition of good things from God."* [20]

Primarily, the conversation with God as a spiritual activity is emphasized. However, there is also the practice and the experience that not only thoughts, conversation and spiritual acts on their own are included in prayer, but so is the body. Prayer becomes more complete by means of the body and the movement, which accompanies the words of prayer. The body and its movement support prayer making it more complete and expressive so that it may more easily encompass the entire person.

The unification of the body and soul in prayer are particularly manifested in fasting and prayer. The physical fast makes prayer more complete. A person, who fasts, prays better and a person, who prays, fasts more easily. In this way, prayer does not only remain an expression or words, but includes the entire human being. Physical fasting is an admission to God before men that one cannot do it alone and needs help. A person experiences his helplessness more easily when he fasts and that is why, by means of the physical fast, the soul is more open to God. Without fasting, our words of prayer remain without a true foundation. In the Old Testament the faithful fasted and prayed individually, in groups and in various life situations. Because of this, they always experienced God's help. (cf. Ezr 8,21-23; 2 Chr 20,12) Jesus ascribes a special power to fasting and prayer, especially in the battle against evil spirits. (cf. Mk 9,29) The same practice is found in the tradition of the Catholic Church and is most evident in the rules of all orders and religious communities. St. Bernard wrote about the relationship between fasting and prayer saying:

"I will tell you something that you will understand easily and what you have often experienced, if I am not mistaken: fasting gives certainty to prayer and makes it

---

[20] *Catechism of the Catholic Church*, p. 554., no. 2559.

fervent . . . By means of prayer strength is gained for fasting and through fasting the grace of prayer. Fasting strengthens prayer and prayer strengthens fasting and offers it to the Lord." [21]

This is apparent because by means of fasting, one becomes more awake and open to God and to what is spiritual. For the same reason, fasting is connected to the Eucharist. While a person practices renunciation and lives for a period of time with bread, he prepares himself for a meeting with the Divine Bread. This exceptional meeting with God, especially in connection with the Eucharist, is evidence of how fasting is positive in itself and how it enables us to realize the fundamental goal of prayer - the meeting of the entire person with God, the Savior.

In our time, Gandhi is known as a man who fasted and prayed. He said, *"My religion teaches me that in every affliction which cannot be alleviated, it is necessary to fast and pray."* [22] Although it is known that Gandhi fasted and prayed with political goals in mind, he deeply believed that only God could change the heart and man's intentions through fasting and prayer. He believed that with fasting and prayer, man is purified within and frees himself from guilt, which, at the same time, is an expression of solidarity with those who suffer.

From the above, it must be concluded that fasting and prayer are inseparable just as man as a whole, comprised of the spirit, soul and body, is inseparable.

10.6. Fasting and The Eucharist

It is a fact that Jesus established the Eucharist at the solemn Paschal feast. He gave His Apostles His Body for food and His Blood for drink at the Last Supper for the first time. However, from the beginning of the Church, the faithful prepared themselves for the meeting with Christ in the Eucharist, by way of the 'Eucharist fast'.

---

[21] Grün, *Fasten*, p. 40.
[22] *Ibid*, p. 38.

In the original Church tradition (which is recognized even today in the Eastern Church communities that are also geographically closer to the beginning of the Church), the spirit, which governed from the beginning, is visible. This way of preparation can be recognized in the Orthodox Church. Those preparing for Communion have a program of fasting for the entire week. That program becomes stricter as the day of Communion draws near. Unfortunately, they seldom receive Communion.

We must not forget that daily Communion was not always permitted. The Church rule stated that it is necessary to confess annually and to receive Communion at Easter. When the possibility of more frequent Communion was introduced, the rule provided that even water could not be taken from midnight until the moment of Communion. Only the taking of medicine was permitted. The Liturgical Renewal which commenced during the time of Pope Pius XII permitted the celebration of Holy Mass in the afternoon and the Eucharistic fasting, for practical reasons, was reduced to three hours. After the Second Vatican Council, the Eucharistic fast was reduced to one hour before Communion. Because of this, practically speaking, the preparation for the Eucharist by means of fasting has actually disappeared.

The problem is not in the reduction of the length of the Eucharistic fast itself. The problem is that there is no appropriate preparation for the meeting with Christ in the Eucharist. A real danger exists that the deep reverence for Christ's presence in the Eucharist is being lost. With it, the true differentiation between the ordinary bread and the Eucharistic Bread are likewise being lost. In speaking about the Eucharistic celebration of the community in Corinth, along with other things, St. Paul writes:

"A person should examine himself, and so eat the bread and drink the cup. For anyone who eats and drinks

without discerning the body, eats and drinks judgment on himself." (1 Cor 11,28-29)

I am convinced that the Eucharistic fast was actually the door through which one entered into the Mystery of Christ's Presence with deep respect, distinguishing ordinary bread from the Body of Christ. How important was the expectation of the meeting with Christ for children receiving First Communion! For this meeting, they prepared themselves with a strict fast from midnight to the moment of receiving Communion. By this fast, the souls of the faithful were led into the Mystery of the wondrous Presence of Christ in the Eucharist. The danger of a superficial meeting with the Eucharistic Christ was also more easily avoided. When a believer starts to meet Christ in the Eucharist without preparation for this meeting with Him, the true relationship between Christ, Who has remained with His people in the Bread, and the person who receives Him in Communion, is lost.

The fact that Our Lady calls us to a two day fast, on Wednesdays and Fridays, in its own way attests to a preparation for a meeting with the Eucharistic Christ. Thursday has always been a day of the Eucharist and the Priesthood. This is why the Wednesday fast, from the Eucharistic standpoint, is in preparation for Thursday, the day of the Eucharist. The Friday fast is in thanksgiving for the Eucharist and is a realization of the possibility of remaining with the Eucharistic Christ for an entire lifetime.

By worthily preparing for the meeting with the Eucharistic Christ at the Eucharistic feast, man prepares himself for the eternal feast in Heaven. In its own way, the Eucharist is a preparation and a foretaste of the eternal feast in the Kingdom of God.

10.7. Fasting and Good Works

Already in the Old Testament, it is emphasized that it is not sufficient to fast and pray. Instead, through fasting and prayer man, as a believer, must be made capable of good works. This is why fasting, prayer and good works always go together and are a condition of each other. The one who fasts and prays will become free to realize what he has, what he needs, and what he can give to others to do with as they will. The aim is not so much to place what one has and does not use for the use of the poor, as it is for man's demands to be reduced to their proper measure. If a person does not fast and pray, his needs will continuously increase and he will not be able to control them. The more we need, the less we have to give to others. We become agitated, violent, avaricious, miserly and unjust about many things that we are convinced we need but do not have. It can be said that others convinced us that we must have them. This is especially a great danger today when through the media, and particularly television, something new is continually being offered. In order to be able to follow the rhythm of the world, man is forced to work more, to 'spend' his life, to neglect his spiritual values and family and even to destroy his own life. In such an environment, neither does man see what he has, nor what he needs, nor what he can leave to the disposition of others.

Through fasting a person becomes capable of seeing more clearly so that his relationship with material things can change. In particular, the value of fasting and prayer is measured by a change in such a relationship and in an end to the race for material goods. Sensitivity to the situation of others and a readiness to help are the main criteria for fasting and prayer. If someone fasts and prays without his sense of responsibility growing and without being prepared to do something about it, the value of his fasting and prayer is brought into question. Someone who fasts and prays must become generous, merciful and sensitive to others. He must be able to recognize Christ in the poor, the misfortunate and the needy. He must do everything he can for others out of love for Christ, Who has identified Himself with each one of us, especially with the poor and the needy.

10.8. Fasting and Prayer Against Demonic Forces

It does not seem accidental that as fasting has been forgotten in the Church, in some way, the battle against demonic forces has also been forgotten. As talk about fasting in the Church has nearly disappeared, the fight against Satan and his kingdom has also disappeared. While Satanic works are becoming more evident in the world – in Satanic groups, books, films, songs, rock groups who in their songs attest to be slaves of Satan and even in construction of temples to Satan – in the past decades in the Church, Satanic influence has become a theme that is not spoken of. Even exorcism, the service of deliverance from Satanic forces which Jesus entrusted to the Apostles, has also disappeared. (cf. Mt 7,22; 10,8 etc.)

However, where Mary is accepted as the Mother of the Church and Its Teacher, this battle is not forgotten but continues. This is also not accidental. I recall a conversation with Monsignor Milingo who is well known for consciously living Jesus' commandment and for his priestly authority over evil spirits in his service of deliverance. In that conversation he said something about Our Lady that I never heard before. He said that Our Lady was the first exorcist because after the original sin, She was presented as the Woman with Child Who battled against Satan. Satan was to strike at Her heel, but She would crush his head. (cf. Gn 3,15)

The book of Revelations speaks about the Woman Who is about to give birth: Satan wanted to devour Her child, but She fled into the desert and saved Him. (cf. Rv 12,2-6)

I recall my own experience in praying over individuals who I could gather were under the influence of Satan. While praying over them, abusive words against Jesus, against the Cross, against the Most Blessed Sacrament of the Altar and, without exception, against Mary, the Mother of Jesus, could be heard. If She is the One Who is to crush Satan's head and defeat him, then it is normal for him to rebel and fight against Her.

The service of exorcism that has been neglected and forgotten over the course of past years is again being introduced into the Church. While many dioceses have again named priests with special authority in this service, unfortunately, many have not yet done so. This practice is being renewed because an increasing number of faithful feel the presence of evil spirits or are themselves obsessed and seek help from a priest. If the priests do not help, the faithful then turn to fortune-tellers and various other so-called healers who cast them further into evil.

Through the entire history of the Church, all exorcist priests prepared themselves for the prayer of exorcism by fasting and praying. This is also being renewed today. Many of today's exorcists are surrounded by people who fast and pray together with them. Not only do they accompany them in preparation but also during the prayer itself. This has shown itself to be very good and beneficial as a protection for the priest himself, for the person who is being prayed over and for society in general.

Recently an International Association of Exorcists, which includes an increasing number of priests, has been established. In order to justify all this, we need to recall the words of St. Peter:

"Be sober and vigilant. Your opponent the devil is prowling around like a roaring lion looking for someone to devour." (1 Pt 5,8)

This is why I am including an interview with an exorcist priest, Fr. Martin Ramoser, who is responsible for the German-speaking region. His knowledge and experience, as well as his journey to this service can help us better understand and accept this matter.

Interview with Father Martin Ramoser

I must admit that I only knew him to see him. We would always greet each other but, I knew nothing more about him. Among other things, it surprised me that for the previous few years he had spent all of his vacations in Medjugorje for his own reasons. I was especially surprised to hear that he is responsible for the service of deliverance (previously called service of exorcism) in Germany. I asked him for this interview and am grateful to him for everything that he has shared with us from the wealth of his experience.

Father Martin, please introduce yourself to our readers.

I am Martin Ramoser, a parish priest in Resibeck in a Bavarian diocese of Regensburg. I am 46 years old and have been a priest for 20 years. I come from south Bavaria some 20 miles away from Altöting. My father was a blacksmith and I have a sister. We had a small farm. My life's journey, and my way to the priesthood, developed normally. I was a chaplain for 5 years and then became a parish priest.

You mentioned that in Germany you are responsible for the service of liberation. How is it, that at a time like this, when not much is spoken about exorcism you entered into this type of 'work'?

There are many reasons for this. First I began to participate in the Charismatic renewal. In my parish community, I met an anorexic girl who tried to commit suicide several times. A family lived with me in my parish office when I came to know her and her situation, which was catastrophic. I accepted her into the parish office but despite all my efforts, I could not help her. One day she went to stay with a family belonging to a 'free' church and six months later, she experienced deliverance. I was really angry about this fact and thought, "A man who left the Church and became a member of some free church was able to help this girl while I, a Catholic priest, was not able to help her." Afterwards several other people left our parish community and joined that free church. They also found real spiritual renewal there and not with me. This confused me somewhat.

Then in my parish, a prayer group started. They preferred to stay more in contact with the people from the free church than with me, their parish priest, even though they were all my friends. I organized various pilgrimages with them. One day I said to myself, "I have to enter this prayer group and return people to the Catholic Church because they are going the wrong way." The first time I came to the prayer group, the leader of the free church who helped my anorexic parishioner to be healed, sat next to me. I was about to explode even though he was so nice to me. This made me even more angry. In that prayer group, I experienced how individuals were praying for each other and especially for the sick. I heard them in the name of Jesus commanding illnesses and evil spirits to leave people and I saw some people experiencing real help.

Once I participated in this prayer group several times, the prejudices in my soul started slowly to melt away. I also came to experience a special strength that was present there which we neglected in the Catholic Church, namely, the acknowledgement that the powers of darkness exist, and that in the name of Jesus we have power and authority over these forces and are permitted to command them. It did not take long for me to understand that I had to look for this in the Catholic Church so as not to be led to the free church. I was healed of a back problem I had when one of the members of the free church prayed over me.

Is it not said, "He who believes in Jesus and invokes His name. . .?"

Yes, but I was labeled as practicing free theology which was very modern in Germany in my time! In any event, I started to look for what I experienced in the free church in the Catholic Church. I found prayer groups that practiced the prayer of deliverance.

How did it come about that you are in the service of deliverance now?

Somehow, everything proceeded normally. In 1995, I participated in a seminar for healing led by Fr. Emilian Tardif in San Giovanni Rotondo. Afterwards, there was a conference of the IAD and a service of deliverance with Fr. Rufus Pereira. I remained in contact with the IAD and as of then became its representative in the German-speaking region. I am now convinced that this service of deliverance must again become a conscious part of priestly service.

What does IAD stand for?

This is an abbreviation for the International Association for Deliverance. The situation is such that in many countries like Germany there are two extremes. In the first extreme the existence of Satan and demons generally is denied; evil is seen as something impersonal, an energy and Satan is claimed not to exist. For this reason, problems are confined to the area of Psychology. When someone experiences special problems, priests and Bishops send them to psychiatrists. The service of deliverance has completely disappeared. In Germany, there is a well-known case of 'Klingenberg'. It was a situation in which the service of deliverance did not succeed. The girl died and the exorcists ended up in jail. Because of this, Bishops and priests are afraid of similar situations and don't want to have anything to do with them. This is the first extreme.

The other extreme comes through New Age, Satanic cults, rock music, Far East practices, such as Reiki, and through many other things. Many people enter into the unfamiliar Satanic areas and distance themselves from the Church. A question is asked of us, "How can these people be helped?" In Italy there is a widespread problem of witches, magic and curses. Because of this, many Bishops in the dioceses have again appointed exorcists to combat these problems. This still has not happened in other countries. Bishops do not permit priests to be involved with these problems. Because of this, the International Association for Deliverance has come into being with Fr. Rufus Periera as its Vice-President. Both priests and lay people participate equally in this association.

How can fear and the negative position of the Bishops and priests be understood when it is known that Jesus gave the power to the priests to proclaim the Good News, to forgive sins, to heal the sick and to cast out evil spirits?

I believe that there are several reasons for this. This negative stance towards the service of deliverance came about at the age of enlightenment and then as a result of Freemasonry and New Age. The spirit of these movements and positions entered the Church. It was claimed that these were notions of the 'middle ages' which have been overcome; and that the expression 'powers of darkness' needs to be understood symbolically because they do not exist at all. Bishops are afraid of being ridiculed by the press and of being labeled as 'backwards' and from the 'middle ages' if they believe in something like that. Many Bishops have a great fear of this.

Can you recall a certain event that has convinced you of Satan, demons and that demonic forces exist?

I can describe a situation I experienced last year. A family from southern Bavaria called me to come and see them because Fr. Jörg Müller recommended me. It was a matter of a four-year-old child who regularly woke up at night, about an hour after going to sleep. He would get out of bed, look into the corner and with an adult voice, would make strange sounds and look completely disturbed. When the parents asked him what this was all about, he answered, "I am not allowed to say who it was, but it was someone." The boy experienced deep fears. The fact that the child spoke in a deep, dismal voice of an adult man was very strange. The doctors were not able to help. Then, three of us from IAD came. First of all, we assessed the situation. From our experience, we know that one cannot immediately

118

presume that it is a matter of Satan. We must discern carefully what is actually happening. Since man is made in the image of God, he has three dimensions: the soul, the spirit and the body. Today it is fashionable to speak about psychosomatic illnesses while the third spiritual dimension is forgotten or excluded altogether. First it must be established whether it is a psychosomatic, psychiatric or a spiritual matter. In search for the truth, it is also necessary to examine all the circumstances in which something is taking place.

While we were carrying out our investigation, on one occasion, the boy again began to shout. Immediately we went into the bedroom and started to pray. While the other two prayed silently, I was praying the prayer of exorcism in Latin. Although the boy was not in a waking state, several times, at special points of prayer, he jumped towards me, grabbed me by my stole and tried to push me away. He was in a state of some kind of a trance. I prayed the Baptismal exorcism six or seven times and the manifestation diminished. We prayed once more and everything calmed down. In that, I experienced that the powers of darkness react when they are countered with prayer and they must withdraw.

It often happens that obsessed individuals start raging and thrashing around with their legs and arms when we pray. After prayer, they are not conscious of their behavior at all, although they were awake. They fall into such states only during the time of prayer. Such behavior confirms that the powers of darkness exist.

What is important with regard to discernment and who helps you in that?

There is another married couple with me. First, we ask for a description of the manifestation: when it started, the personal circumstances and the circumstances concerning the close and extended family. It is particularly important to know if there are any special problems; whether, for example, someone, even in previous generations, practiced in magic. We always ask whether there were suicides, abortions, unjust divisions of land and inheritances and any curses connected with them.

What do you do if you find that something extends beyond the psychosomatic level?

Very often all three levels are together: physical and psychological symptoms with the spiritual. This is why we pray for inner healing in addition to deliverance. In preparation for praying over the person in question, the three of us pray together. We always pray, conscious of the power Jesus gave to the Church, by invoking His Name and asking for deliverance or we pray the Baptismal exorcism. I do not pray the Great Exorcism because the Bishop has not yet officially appointed me as an exorcist. In the name of Jesus, I command the powers of darkness to withdraw and I always pray for healing. It is very important for the person in question to continue to grow in faith.

You had mentioned New Age, Reiki and Eastern meditations before. Do these practices and ideologies contain anything Satanic?

Unfortunately, yes. The father of the boy I spoke about, taught Reiki. I actually consider this to be the cause of that manifestation. He finally saw his mistake and renounced every contact with Reiki. He also publicly promised not to practice it again and publicly told his successor, who passed all levels to become a teacher, that all of this was wrong and dangerous. When Fr. Rufus Pereira came to visit us, he prayed over him. After doing so, he admitted that he felt some force leave that man.

What is 'Reiki'?

Behind Reiki stands the Gnostic concept that healing comes when cosmic energies are invoked upon a person. Individuals who, through special exercises, have become mediums of cosmic energy said to have healing power do this. The healing does not come from an individual but from an energy which that individual is enabled to invoke by laying on of hands. Teachers of Reiki confirm that there are healings. Since this does not take place in the name of Jesus, space is opened for demonic powers, which afflict individuals and families.

What do you recommend to those who have experienced deliverance in the name of Jesus?

It is most important for them to try to live a Christian life of faith and for them to remain with Christ. Because when a healing and deliverance take place without the person living a Christian life, things can get even worse. Jesus said that if the evil spirit is cast out but the house remains empty, seven other spirits, worse than the one that has been cast out, can enter. It is important to deepen the personal relationship with Christ. I recommend that priests become involved in combating these manifestations; for them to help people to be delivered by the power of the Holy Spirit and to live a Christian life.

Everyone in this service tends to speak about rock music as something very dangerous for the spiritual life?

Today there are many channels through which evil forces can creep into man. According to my experience, one of them is rock music. Certainly, the powers of darkness find 'open windows' also through such music to influence man. I recall a well-known group AC/DC. One of their best-known songs gives glory to Satan and is called 'Highway to Hell'. The refrain says, "hey Satan, paid my due, playin' in a rockin' band. Hey mama look at me, I'm on my way to the promised land and I'm going down, all the way down. I'm on the Highway to hell, on the highway to hell..." When a person repeats this or a similar text, his soul is opened to dark forces. This is why it is important for all of us, especially the young, to pray the Rosary because in the Rosary, we repeat the 'Hail Mary' many times. In this way, we slowly open ourselves to Salvation just as we open ourselves to evil when we repeat negative things. I especially recommend to the young who listen to similar such music to pray the Rosary often or to repeat, 'Father, Your Kingdom come, Hallowed be Your Name'.

The shortest prayer of deliverance is found in the prayer of Our Father: 'Deliver us from evil'.

Do you see Mary's call to fasting and prayer as connected with the service of deliverance?

Absolutely! The prayer of the Rosary is a good preparation and by all means so are fasting and regular Confession. If we are not pure, then evil forces can say to us, "What can you do to me when I partake in your life"? The powers of darkness fear the Eucharist and the Word of God. It is clear why the message of Medjugorje, in its entirety, is most efficacious in the fight against evil.

How many times have you been to Medjugorje and why do you come?

This is already the sixth summer that I have spent my entire vacation in Medjugorje. I have also come with my parishioners. I feel that this spirituality is the most suitable for the service of deliverance: the Holy Mass, Confession, the Rosary and the Sacred Scripture. It is also the most suitable help to those who have experienced deliverance. Such a spiritual environment must be experienced by those in the service of deliverance and those in need of deliverance.

Did you have difficulty in accepting Medjugorje?

At the beginning, I had many difficulties, but after my second conversion, I no longer have them.

Your second conversion?

Yes. As I said at the beginning, I was in a very difficult crisis because of a situation with that girl I was unable to deliver. She experienced her deliverance in the free church when members of the prayer group prayed over her by invoking the name of Jesus. It is clear to me that Medjugorje's spirituality is a great gift for our time because it is here that one enters into a personal relationship with Christ through the Sacraments and many prayers. Whoever remains united with Jesus and

Mary in the faith of the Church is best protected from evil and remains free.

According to your experience, what role does Mary have in the service of deliverance?

So many times, I have experienced Mary to be the best helper in the fight against the powers of darkness. Whenever I have invoked Mary, giving glory to Her Immaculate Conception and Her Divine Motherhood during the prayer of deliverance, the powers of darkness had to flee. A French exorcist, a member of the Association of Exorcists, said that many times his experience confirmed that the evil spirits fear Mary even more than they fear Jesus. Somehow, this can be understood on a human level. The evil spirits must submit to Jesus, but to submit to a humble Woman is their greatest shame.

Do you have anything else to say to us?

I am grateful to God for Mary's messages and for everything that is happening in Medjugorje. I am convinced that God decided to create conditions through Mary to deliver us from the evil one.

10.9. The Gospel of Life - Pope John Paul II

It is very important to understand that there is not a single Medjugorje message that is not founded on Sacred Scripture. There is also nothing new in Medjugorje in a liturgically-pastoral sense that would need to wait for special Church approval. This is why it is important to do everything Our Lady is asking of us, without waiting for an official approval of Medjugorje. Even if there were no apparitions, no mistake has been made by those who started to fast and pray more, go to Confession, read Sacred Scripture, Adore Jesus in the Most Holy Sacrament of the Altar, Venerate the Cross and pray for healing after Mass. These are all the things that have been done day in and day out in Medjugorje. However, the fact that this is happening is in itself the best proof of a supernatural intervention of God's grace. Everything that is taking place started the day the visionaries said that Our Lady appeared and called us to peace, to conversion, to fasting, to prayer, to renewal of faith, to celebration of Holy Mass, to Confession, to Adoration and to reading of Sacred Scripture.

Even though, generally speaking, fasting has been forgotten in the Church, Pope John Paul II has called us to fast. He himself fasted and prayed for a day in Assisi together with the responsible leaders of other religions. In his document, 'The Gospel of Life', he speaks about fasting and calls us to fasting and prayer. He emphasizes that the best way of fighting against Satan and his kingdom is by fasting and prayer.

In number 100 of the 'Gospel of Life' he states:

"In this great endeavor to create a new culture of life we are inspired and sustained by the confidence that comes from knowing that the Gospel of life, like the Kingdom of God itself, is growing and producing abundant fruit. (cf. Mk 4:26-29) There is certainly an enormous disparity between the powerful resources available to the forces promoting the "culture of death" and the means at the disposal of those working for a "culture of life and love." But we know that we can rely on the help of God, for whom nothing is impossible. (cf. Mt 19:26)

Filled with this certainty, and moved by profound concern for the destiny of every man and woman, I repeat what I said to those families who carry out their challenging mission amid so many difficulties: (135) a great prayer for life is urgently needed, a prayer which will rise up throughout the world. Through special initiatives and in daily prayer, may an impassioned plea rise to God, the Creator and lover of life, from every Christian community, from every group and association, from every family and from the heart of every believer. Jesus himself has shown us by his own example that prayer and fasting are the first and most effective weapons against the forces of evil. (cf. Mt 4:1-11) As he taught his disciples, some demons cannot be driven out except in this way. (cf. Mk 9:29) Let us therefore discover anew the humility and the courage to pray and fast so that power from on high will break down the walls of lies and deceit: the walls which conceal from the sight of so many of our brothers and sisters the evil of practices and laws which are hostile to life. May this same power turn their hearts to resolutions and goals inspired by the civilization of life and love." [23]

10.10. 'Paenitemini'–Pope Paul VI

By all means, the Apostolic constitution concerning fasting and penance issued by Pope Paul VI must be mentioned.[24] In the very introduction of the document, Pope Paul VI sets out the reason for its publication, namely, the necessity to teach all those with religious insight about penance.

This teaching pertains to the content and the meaning of God's commandment to do penance. The Church, in itself, bears what is human and divine, what is visible and invisible, and what is passing and permanent. Jesus Himself connected the proclamation of the Gospel with penance. He started His preaching by a call to penance and conversion and a call to faith in the Gospel, the Good News. John the Baptist prepared himself for his assignment by strict penance of fasting and renunciation. (cf. Mk 1,1) The very coming of Jesus is seen by St. Paul as a divestment, a renunciation of the Divine; of His equality with God. Jesus became a slave like other men. (cf. Phil 2,6) A Christian is called to partake in Christ's mission and so must take upon himself everything Jesus did. This includes fasting, prayer, and everything Jesus taught. Christ's Passion and Death on the Cross must be seen in this light.

Although the Church is holy, without stain or wrinkle, it is comprised of individuals who are sinful. This is why It continually calls to conversion, to penance and to

---

[23] *The Gospel of Life*, Pope John Paul II, Rome, at St. Peter's, March 25, 1995., especially number 100.

[24] *PAENITEMINI* (Apostolic Constitution On Penance), Pope Paul VI, Issued on February 17, 1966.

fasting. One of the essential assignments of the Church, as teacher, is to proclaim penance and to teach its members how to free themselves from their attachments to material things. This is so that the faithful on their life's journey toward the heavenly homeland may not be stopped nor close themselves to divine work and cooperation with God.

Penance must be done for interior purification and for forgiveness of sins. (cf. Acts 2,38) This is emphasized as a condition for an interior life with God. Further on in the document, various Biblical situations are noted where penance and fasting were practiced. The main criterion for what is done externally is the interior process, which must take place when practicing penance and fasting. In this context, the document speaks about external forms that change according to the circumstances of time and space in which people live. The Church determines various exercises of penance at the general level. The Bishops are responsible for the forms of penance in their dioceses and parish priests in their parishes. While respecting the ordinances and the direction of the general Church, it is necessary for the forms of such penance to be appropriate to the region the faithful reside in.

When we compare internal processes and the meaning of fasting and penance with external references about penance and forms of penance, it is easy to see that more has remained of the external aspect of fasting and penance. This is understandable because the external aspect is visible, it can be measured and evaluated and depends on the free choice of the believer. On the other hand, the internal process is beyond the influence of the human will since it is a fruit of grace united with man's cooperation.

The first virtuous exercise of penance is actually the conscious fulfillment of the obligations the believer has in his life, which demand patience and a daily faithfulness to the end. Believers who are struck by difficulties of illness, of poverty and of persecution are called to unite their pain with Christ's; this being their virtuous exercise of penance.

"The precept of penitence must be satisfied in a more perfect way by priests, who are more closely linked to Christ through sacred character, as well as by those who in order to follow more closely the abnegation of the Lord and to find an easier and more efficacious path to the perfection of charity practiced by the evangelical counsels. Christ abdicated his divine image so as to in this way more easily and efficaciously reach perfection of love." [25]

In addition to the above noted general call to the virtue of penance, the believers are encouraged to accept and practice the mortification of the body.[26]

Despite the freedom in the ordinances pertaining to fasting and penance, and the fact that the Pope desires that there be freedom in individual situations, it is his desire that some things should remain in common in order to unite the faithful of the Catholic Church. For this reason, ordinances uniting all the faithful are found at the end of the constitution.

First of all, it is said that by divine law all the faithful are required to do penance. So far as prescriptions of ecclesiastical law regarding penitence are concerned, the time of Lent preserves its penitential character, as does every Friday throughout the year. On such days, abstinence is to be observed while Ash Wednesday and Good Friday remain days of strict abstinence and fasting. The law of abstinence forbids the use of meat and it is obligatory for all the faithful who are over 14 years of age. The law of fasting allows only one full meal a day, but does not prohibit taking less food in the morning and evening according to local custom. Those faithful between 21 and 60 years of age are bound by the law of fasting. It is up to the Bishops and then parish priests to establish the norms which, in their pastoral

---

[25] *Paenitemini*, p. 35
[26] *Ibid*, 37

prudence and knowledge of local conditions, they consider the most opportune and efficacious. [27]

When what is said in this Apostolic constitution is compared with the practice of the Old and New Testaments and with the tradition of the Church and closed orders of the Church, it is easy to notice that fasting and penance were brought to the level where they were easily lost. This is what has happened.

---

[27] *Paenitemini*, p. 44

XI. FASTING AND RELIGIONS

It would be difficult to try to encompass the general practice of fasting of the religions of the world. One thing, however, is certain. Every religious practice, starting with the oldest, knows fasting and its practice. The times of fasting and the situations of fasting vary, but the goal has always been the same: to create better conditions for a better relationship with God and with what is Divine.

All founders of religions fasted. In addition to the religious dimension of fasting, its importance for mental and physical health has been discovered. This is confirmed by an old proverb: "Fasting is food for the soul. It curtails the intemperance of the tongue and seals the lips; it reduces the desire for pleasure and calms the colic temperament; it helps in discernment and gives vigor to the body; it frees from nightmares, heals headaches and strengthens eyesight." [28] [29]

Fasting was also seen to be of great value by the ancient Greeks and Romans. The Greek word for fasting which is also used in the New Testament is 'nestuo' which means not to take food, not to eat anything and to be sober. The expression 'hagnos' is also used and means to have reverential fear, to awaken the religious sentiment of reverential fear. The Latin expression 'ieiunare' also means not to eat. In the Old Testament the word used for fasting, 'som', connects the practice of fasting with the religious experience.[30]

All Eastern Christian churches and communities, like the entire tradition of the Catholic Church, know fasting, which continues to be lost in the West. The Eastern

---

[28] Buchinger, O. i A., *Das Heilende Fasten*, Dr. Werner Jopp Verlag, Wiesbaden, 1991., p. 16

[29] *Ibid*, p. 29

[30] Cf. *Theologische Realenzyklopödie*, Edition XI, Berlin - New York, 1983., pg. 42-59. und *Reallexikon für Antike und Christentum*, Edition VII, Stuttgart, 1969., pg. 443-524.

Churches have remained more faithful to the fasting of the first Christian community, namely, to the Jewish fast.

In the Islamic world, fasting is emphasized and it can be verified that those belonging to the Islamic faith have remained faithful to the rules of fasting.

I should like to note here the fact that, so far as teaching is concerned, the Orthodox Church has not forgotten the meaning of fasting. In preparation for their great and holy Council, Pre-council conferences are held. On November 6, 1986, the third such conference was held in Chambesy, Switzerland. Along with other texts, the concluding text quoted here was proclaimed:

"Fasting is a commandment of God. (cf. Gn 2,16-17) According to St. Basil the Great, "fasting is as old as man because it was ordered in Heaven." (about fasting 1,3) Fasting is a great spiritual exercise and an exceptional expression of the ascetic ideal of Orthodoxy. In that the Orthodox Church faithfully follows the Apostolic teaching, the Canon of Synod and the entire patriarchal tradition; it has always emphasized the great value of fasting for the spiritual life of man and his Salvation. During the course of the entire liturgical year, the Church mediates on the whole of the patriarchal tradition and teaching about fasting as a pre-condition essential for man to reach incessant and permanent vigilance and inextinguishable fervor in the spiritual battle. That is why, in the Church, fasting is spoken about as a divine gift, a light of grace, an unconquerable weapon, the foundation of spiritual battle; an excellent way toward good, food for the soul, proof of God's help, source of meditation, an example of and incorrupt way of life similar to the way of the angels, the 'mother of all good and every virtue' and as an image of the life to come . . .

Like a caring mother, the Orthodox Church has determined what serves to advance the salvation of man and has introduced the holy times of fasting as a 'protective sign' given from God, of the new life of the faithful in Christ against every deceit of the power of the enemy. Following in the footsteps of the Church fathers, the Church protects the Apostolic statutes, the Canons of the Council and the holy tradition. It always offers the holy times of fasting to the faithful as an exceptional means on the way of their spiritual perfection and salvation. It emphasizes to its faithful the need to uphold the determined times of fasting during the course of the Church year: forty days before Easter; on Wednesdays and Fridays according to the witness of the Holy Canon; before Christmas; before the feast of the Holy Apostles, Peter and Paul; and before the feast of the Assumption of the Mother of God. As well, days of vigil are emphasized before the feast of the Exaltation of the Cross, the feast of the Epiphany and the Beheading of St. John the Baptist, in addition to all other days determined in pastoral care or which the faithful have personally decided to uphold.

Additionally, all the faithful must fast before Holy Communion. They must become accustomed to fast as a sign of penance, in fulfillment of spiritual vows, in accomplishment of a goal and in times of trial. They are to connect fasting with prayer to God in times of trial, before Baptism (of adults), before Ordination, when Church discipline must be fulfilled, on pilgrimages and in other similar circumstances."

The value that the Orthodox Church places on fasting with respect to the renewal of Christian life is clearly visible from this text. [31]

---

[31] Seeger, Hans-Karl *Heilfasten – das Leben neu bedenken*, Butzon & Bercker, Kevelaer, 1988., pp. 40-43.

XII. PRAYER ON FAST DAYS

OUR LADY CALLS

"I would like the people to pray along with me these days. And to pray as much as possible! And to fast strictly on Wednesdays and Fridays and every day to pray at least one Rosary: the joyful, sorrowful and glorious mysteries."

(Message of August 14, 1984)

12.1. Prayer To Begin a Fast Day

O Lord God, You are the Creator of the entire world and my Creator! Today I thank You for having so wonderfully arranged the world. Thank You for the fruitfulness that you have bestowed on mother earth for it to bear such a vast variety of fruit. Thank You for the food prepared from the fruits of the earth. Father, I rejoice with Your creatures; I rejoice today with all the fruit and I give You thanks. O Lord, thank You for our need for the daily bread and for the need of daily drink.

Father Thank You for having created my organism to be able to use the fruit of the earth so as to grow and to serve You. Thank You; Father, for all those who, by their labor, provide new possibilities for life on earth. Thank You for all those who have much and give to others. Thank You for all those who hunger for the Heavenly Bread as they eat the bread of this earth. Father, I also thank You for all those who have nothing to eat today because I am convinced You will send them help through the goodness of others.

Father, today I resolve to fast. In doing so, I do not despise your creatures. I do not renounce them; I only want to rediscover their worth. I have decided to fast because Your prophets fasted, because Your Son Jesus Christ fasted and because His Apostles and Disciples fasted. I especially decide to fast because Your servant and Our Mother, Mary, also fasted. She calls me to fast:

"Dear children! Today I call on you to begin fasting with the heart. There are many people who are fasting, but only because everyone else is fasting. It has become a custom that no one wants to stop. I ask the parish to fast out of gratitude because God has allowed me to stay this long in this parish. Dear children, fast and pray with the heart. Thank you for having responded to my call." (September 20, 1984)

Father, I present this day of fasting to You. Through fasting, I want to listen to Your Word and to live It more fully. During this day, I want to learn to be turned more toward You, despite everything that surrounds me. With this fast, which I take freely upon myself, I pray to You for all those who are hungry and who, because of their hunger, have become aggressive.

I offer this fast to You for peace in the world. Wars come about because we are attached to material things and are even ready to kill each other because of them. Father I offer this fast to You for all those who are completely bound to material things so they are unable to see any other value.

I pray for all those who are in conflict because they have become blind to what they have. Father by means of this fast open their eyes to what You have given to us and to what we have.

I repent for my blindness that has taken a hold of my senses and prevents me from thanking You for the good that I have. I repent for every abuse of material possessions when I have wrongly evaluated their worth.

Enable me to hear Your word better. Today, through this fast, may my love for You and my neighbors grow.

Father, I have decided to live on bread and water today in order to understand better the value of the Heavenly Bread, and the presence of Your Son in the Eucharist. Let my faith and trust grow through fasting. Father, I have decided to fast and I accept fasting because I know that my yearning for You will grow in this way. Eagerly and with gratitude, I think of Your Son's words, "Blessed are the poor in spirit, the reign of God is theirs."

Father; make me poor before You. Through fasting, grant me the grace to understand how much I need You. Grant that through fasting my desire for You may grow; that my heart may yearn for You as the deer yearns for running waters; as the desert longs for clouds of rain.

Father, I pray to You – that through this fast especially my understanding for the hungry and the thirsty and for those who do not have enough material goods may grow. Help me see what it is that I possess and do not need so that I may know how to renounce such possessions for the benefit of my brothers and sisters.

O, Father, I especially ask You for the grace of awareness that I am but a pilgrim on this earth and that, at the moment of passing to the other world, I shall not take anything with me except love and good works. Grant that awareness may grow within me so that I may know that nothing belongs to me, even when I am in possession of it. I have received everything I have from You only in order to manage it. Father through fasting, grant me the grace to become more humble and more willing to do Your Will. Cleanse me of my selfishness and pride.

Through this fast, cleanse me of all bad habits and still my passions, so that virtue may increase in me. Let the depth of my soul open to Your grace through this fast so that Your grace may totally transform and cleanse me. In trials and temptations, help me to always be like Your Son; to resist every temptation, so that I may be able to serve You and seek Your Word more and more, each passing day.

Mary, You were free in Your heart and bound to nothing except the Father's Will. Obtain for me the grace of a joyful fast today, in which my heart will be able to sing a song of thanksgiving with You. Obtain for me the grace that my decision to fast may be firm and lasting. I offer the difficulties and the hunger I am going to feel today for all people. Mary, pray for me. Let every evil and temptation of Satan be kept away from me today through Your intercession and through the power of Your protection. Mary, teach me to fast and to pray so that day by day, I may become more and more like You and Your Son, Jesus Christ, in the Holy Spirit!   Amen.

12.2. Rosary on a Fast Day

To pray the Rosary means to be with Jesus and Mary, in joy, in sorrow and in glory. When things are going well for us, we easily forget God and then cause problems and difficulties to ourselves and to others. These become real crosses in life. This is why we need the Joyful Mysteries in order to learn how to live with God when things are going well.

When things are difficult, we are inclined to complain to God because of our suffering and we distance ourselves from Him. In suffering we easily lose our faith, hope, love and trust and so live in anguish, fear, bitterness and mistrust. That is why it is good for us to learn how to live when it is difficult for us and why we need the Sorrowful Mysteries.

In order to carry our crosses more easily, we need to be with Jesus and Mary in glory to see what happens after the Cross, the Passion and Death. We often behave like children who see nothing else in a doctor except a painful injection. They cry and want to run away. When a person fixes his sight on healing, he can more easily accept every suffering.

In that sense, I recommend the prayer of the Rosary on a fast day for the grace of fasting and in order to learn how to live with Jesus and Mary.

12.2.1. The Joyful Mysteries

Introductory prayer:

Heavenly Father, Creator of the entire world, I thank You for having called me to pray in union with You in

Your Son Jesus Christ through the Holy Spirit. On this fast day today, I have decided to be with Your Son and His Mother, Mary. I want to live this day joyfully. You are the God of peace and joy; of love and freedom. I surrender my heart to You and I ask You to give me Your Light and Your strength so that I can live this fast day joyfully like Your Son Jesus and like Mary.

The Creed

First Joyful Mystery

Thank You; Father, for announcing Your Will to Mary through the Archangel Gabriel. Thank You, Mary for having an open heart and for placing the Father's Will in the first place in Your life. Thank You for Your response, "Father let it be done to me according to Your Word."

On this fast day, together with You Mary, I ask the Lord to purify my heart of every addiction of this world and from everything, other than God, that has occupied the first place in my heart. I ask Him to free me from everything that has taken away or diminished my inner freedom. I ask Him to free me from everything that has made me blind and deaf in recognizing and accepting His Will. Father, give me the grace on this fast day to recognize and accept Your Will in complete inner freedom, free from all things. Grant that together with Mary, I may say, "Father, let Your Will be done so that You may come to dwell in me completely. "

Our Father, 10 Hail Marys, Glory Be, O my Jesus. . .

Second Joyful Mystery

Mary, when God completely entered into Your life, You were ready to meet others and to bring God into their lives. Thank You for going to visit Elizabeth. Thank You for glorifying the Lord with her and for helping her. In Your heart, You were free and capable of meeting Elizabeth with love. In turn, she was able to recognize God in Your life and was able to bless You. She was able to give glory to Him together with You.

On this fast day, together with You, I ask the Lord to free me from everything that hinders me from meeting others with love. Also, free the hearts of others so that they may recognize the presence of the Lord in me. Through this fasting and prayer today, may my entire being be open to God and to others so that in freedom of heart, I may enter into a joyful communion with them. I offer this day of fasting and prayer for all families so that parents and children may realize the joy of family togetherness in complete inner freedom.

Our Father, 10 Hail Marys, Glory Be, O my Jesus. . .

Third Joyful Mystery

Thank You, Mary, for having given birth to Jesus, the King of Peace, in poverty. You were not embittered by the residents of Bethlehem even though they refused to receive You and Joseph for lodging. They did not want to open their doors even though they saw You with child. You prevailed over bitterness because Your heart was free and secure in the Lord. Thus, the angels were able to sing jubilantly to You because Your heart was joyful.

On this fast day together with You, I ask the Lord to free me from every bond to material things, so that in freedom and love I can joyfully accept the conditions of life in which I live. May I overcome every restlessness to become a person of good will, prepared to accept peace and to proclaim it to others. May my heart be free so that together with You, and like You, I can worship the King of Peace. By the power of fasting and prayer, may the hearts of all those responsible in the Church and in the world become completely free so as to intercede with all their strength for peace for all mankind.

Our Father, 10 Hail Marys, Glory Be, O my Jesus. . .

Fourth Joyful Mystery

Thank You, Mary, for having presented Jesus in the temple for our salvation, together with Joseph, in freedom of heart and with love. May that moment be blessed when the old man Simeon recognized in Your Son the Savior and the Light to illuminate all people. He did so together with Anna who fasted and prayed her entire life.

On this fast day, together with You, I pray to the Lord that through fasting and prayer, all Christians may become capable of encountering Him. May they become capable of recognizing His presence in the Eucharist and in His Word and of meeting Him in every Sacrament with an open and free heart. I am fasting and praying for all those who cannot receive the Lord in their arms like Simeon because their hands are bound by earthly goods and their hearts are turned to the world and its promises. Open all of our hearts and souls so that, in freedom, we may recognize the Lord and celebrate His coming together with Simeon and Anna. Help us, through fasting and prayer, to know how to wait for the Lord and to receive Him when He comes.

Our Father, 10 Hail Marys, Glory Be, O my Jesus. . .

Fifth Joyful Mystery

Thank You, Mary, for having sought and found Your Son in the temple together with Joseph. You were in anguish and sorrow for three full days because You did not know where He was. When You found Him in the temple, Your heart again became quiet in the joy of Your meeting. Jesus, Your Son, did not try to justify Himself but said that He had to be in the house of His Father.

On this fast day, I offer my fasting and prayer, together with You, Mary, for all those who have lost their inner freedom because of poor family upbringing and have wandered far away from the Lord on wrong paths of life in their addiction. Look for them, O Mary, and return them to the house of the Father so that they may live in peace and joy and may grow in love and knowledge before God and man, as Your Son Jesus did in Nazareth.

Our Father, 10 Hail Marys, Glory Be, O my Jesus. . .

Concluding prayer:

Together with Your Son Jesus Christ and the Holy Spirit, I bless You and give glory to You, O Heavenly Father, for giving me the grace to be able to pray and to be with Your Son, Jesus and His Mother Mary on this fast day. Today, through fasting and prayer, may complete peace and joy enter into my heart and into the hearts of all those for whom I fast and pray. Help us to love You more and more even when things are going well for us. Let it be so. Amen.

12.2.2. The Sorrowful Mysteries

Introductory prayer:

Jesus, thank You for coming into the world and for having accepted suffering in order to save it. Give me the grace to discover Your love and Your concern for us men in Your suffering. Grant that I may be grateful for the love with which You suffered for us.

On this fast day, which I want to offer to You in prayer also for the salvation of the world, I especially want to be with You in Your suffering. I want to enter into the Mystery of Your love. I want to accept fasting and prayer with the same love with which You accepted Your fasting and with which You then accepted Your Passion and suffering. I offer my hunger to You today so that You may awaken in me the hunger for the eternal Good, for the Will of the Father, for Your Word, for love and for peace.

Help me, Mary. Teach me to fast and to pray today as You called me to do, so that, like You, I can follow Your Son in His suffering. Amen.

The Creed

First Sorrowful Mystery

Thank You for coming into the Garden of Gethsemane where You prayed, perspired blood and accepted the Will of the Father by accepting the chalice of suffering. Your heart was completely free and that is why You were able to say, "Father, let it be done unto me according to Your Word." You suffered because You loved.

On this fast day, I ask You, Jesus, to give me the grace to fight successfully against my bad habits, which prepare my suffering and anguish. I offer to You all those, who by their addiction to alcohol, drugs and other evils of this world, are preparing difficult moments of Gethsemane for themselves, their families, their spouses and their children. I also offer to You all those who have become criminals because of their addictions and are now imprisoned and suffering a great deal. I also offer to You all those who have destroyed their health because of their addictions. I offer my fasting and prayer for all of them. I thank You for giving inner freedom and peace as well as spiritual, mental and physical health to them all.

Our Father, 10 Hail Marys, Glory Be, O my Jesus. . .

Second Sorrowful Mystery

They bound You to the post in Pilate's court and scourged You mercilessly. Following each strike, wounds remained. Your blood flowed. You were losing strength and You were in pain. You offered all of this for us in order to free us from evil and sin.

On this fast day, reveal to me the love with which You suffered Your scourging so that deep gratitude may come to dwell in my heart for Your suffering. I offer my fasting and prayer for all those who, in their hearts, carry the wounds, they received in their childhood. Because of those wounds they fall into new evils and new addictions, scourging themselves and others. Jesus, break the chain of evil and sin so that Your peace, love and forgiveness may come to dwell in every heart. I offer my fasting and prayers to You for parents who have scourged their children with their drunken behavior, their faithlessness; through drugs, gambling, fights and divorces. Free our families from every lash and evil; free our Church and our people. Grant that all wounds may be healed and all lashes and scourging may cease so that, through fasting and prayer, peace, joy and spiritual and physical health may enter in.

Our Father, 10 Hail Marys, Glory Be, O my Jesus. . .

Third Sorrowful Mystery

Jesus, they crowned You with a crown of thorns to inflict this form of pain upon You also. They pounded the thorns into Your head to ridicule You as a king. They even placed a scarlet cloak upon You and a royal scepter in Your hand. There were those who struck You and spat upon You, pronouncing insults. You suffered all of this in order to redeem us and to free us from evil and from the evil one.

You told us that a kind of evil spirit exists that can only be cast out by fasting and prayer. For this reason, I offer this day of fasting and prayer to You in reparation for all the offenses and humiliations inflicted upon You in black masses and other occult rites. I offer it to You for all those who have joined Satanic sects and have participated in Satanic rites as well as for all those who are involved in spiritism, fortune-telling and spells. In this way, they have fallen under the influence of evil spirits. I offer this day of fasting and prayer to You so that You may free them from Satan and protect them from him because You are the Master. I believe that only one Word from You is sufficient for them to be freed from Satan's power and authority. Only one Word from You is sufficient in order that they enjoy the peace You give. Pronounce this word of deliverance and cast away Satan that he may no longer destroy peace and entice Your people toward the way of damnation.

I offer my fasting and prayer to You for all the priests who have dedicated themselves to the service of deliverance from evil influences. Protect and defend them. Reveal Your power over evil spirits so that such spirits may no longer mislead those whom You have redeemed by Your precious blood.

142

Our Father, 10 Hail Marys, Glory Be, O my Jesus. . .

Fourth Sorrowful Mystery

Jesus, You patiently carried Your Cross; You fell under it and got up again. You continued the way, which You accepted in order to save us. Thank You for each step You took in carrying Your Cross and for each time You fell and got up again. Thank You for Your every encounter on the way of the Cross. You have done everything to save us. Be blessed, praised and glorified through the carrying of Your Cross!

I offer this day of fasting and prayer for all those who are sick and helpless; for all those who are seriously ill and who, in their sickness, have lost every hope. I offer it for all those who serve the sick. I pray to You for parents with sick children who will carry their cross their entire lives. Grant that all may turn to good for them.

Especially, I offer to You those who have destroyed their physical and spiritual health because of overeating or drinking excessively. I offer to You all those who carry the cross of anorexia and bulimia – those who have an unhealthy relationship with food. They both reject food and destroy their health or consume it in excess and then reject it.

I also offer this day of fasting and prayer for all those who are hungry and for malnourished children. Grant that by fasting and prayer, we may be able to share material goods properly.

I also offer this fast day for those who carry the cross of a disorderly relationship in their sexual life; for all homosexuals and lesbians, and for all those who were sexually abused in their childhood. Heal them and free them from every disorderly and unnatural way of life.

Our Father, 10 Hail Marys, Glory Be, O my Jesus. . .

Fifth Sorrowful Mystery

Thank You Jesus for having accepted the Crucifixion and Death on the Cross for us. May You be blessed for that moment when You prayed for Your enemies, when You forgave and when You surrendered Your Spirit to the Father.

I offer this day of fasting and prayer to You for a peaceful passing from this world for myself and everyone else. Through fasting and prayer, may every evil and sin die in me, along with every wrong attachment to myself. May all my unhealthy relationships with myself, with You, with others and with material things, die in me. I offer this day of fasting and prayer to You for all those who have committed suicide and, having completely lost the peace of their souls, have taken their own lives. I offer to You all victims of excessive eating and drinking. I offer to You all those who are perpetrators of violence and have, in their drunkenness, caused road accidents and murders in families. In Your mercy, open the door of eternal life to them. By the power of fasting and prayer may evil and sin die in us so that we may rest in peace in Your eternal Kingdom.

Our Father, 10 Hail Marys, Glory Be, O my Jesus. . .

Concluding prayer:

Thank You Jesus for Your suffering, Your Cross, Your Passion and Your Death. May this fasting and prayer enable me to carry my life's crosses with love so as to give glory to You. On this day of fasting and prayer, grant me the grace to be able to join You in Your Passion with my entire being; with freedom of heart and soul. Grant that I may not be afraid in accepting the cross of fighting against the evil within me and around me so that one day we may all deserve to hear Your words, "Good servant, enter into the eternal feast in the Heavenly Kingdom."

12.2.3. The Glorious Mysteries

Introductory prayer:

I give glory to You, Jesus, for conquering death and rising from the dead. I joyfully exclaim to You, 'Alleluia!' On this day of fasting and prayer grant me the grace to enter into Your glorious victory over sin, evil and death with all my heart and soul, and to experience its beauty. By the power of Your Spirit, remove from my heart everything that does not permit me to enter into the celebration of the great Easter victory with You. Mary, may my heart, like Your Heart, be illuminated with the Risen joy in the early Easter morning.

The Creed

First Glorious Mystery

Jesus, You gloriously rose from the dead. After Your Passion, Cross, Death and Entombment, You came forth victoriously to a new life from the darkness of death and the tomb.

I offer this day of fasting and prayer for myself and for all those who lie in tombs of sin, bad habits, hatred, envy, jealousy, selfishness, pride, godlessness, idolatry and violence. I offer it for all those who, wounded by the sin of others have fallen into dug-out graves. May each heart experience a victorious celebration and give glory and praise to You, O Victorious Jesus.

Our Father, 10 Hail Marys, Glory Be, O my Jesus. . .

Second Glorious Mystery

I give glory to You, Jesus, for having spent forty days with Your Disciples, healing their faith. You gave them peace and prior to Your Ascension, You told them to pray and to wait for the Holy Spirit. You blessed them and then ascended into Heaven.

I offer this day of fasting and prayer for all those who are completely bound to themselves, to others and to material things; for all those who have come to worship the temptation of power so that there is no room for You in their hearts as their gaze is turned towards the world. Through fasting and prayer, may they raise their hearts towards Heavenly goodness so that in the freedom of heart and soul, they can love, forgive, be merciful, be kind, be just and be patient. May the wealthy of this world raise their eyes in the freedom of their hearts to recognize their brothers in the poor and come joyfully to serve them. Through fasting and prayer may the first place in their hearts be for You. May they always remain faithful to You.

Our Father, 10 Hail Marys, Glory Be, O my Jesus. . .

Third Glorious Mystery

I give glory to You Jesus, because, faithful to Your promise, You sent the Holy Spirit upon the Apostles who persevered in prayer together with Mary, Your Mother. They received Him readily and became Your witnesses to the ends of the earth.

I offer this day of fasting and prayer that You may fill the restless with the spirit of peace; the faithless with the spirit of faith; the godless with the spirit of prayer; the weak with the spirit of strength; the foolish with the spirit of wisdom; the sorrowful and anguished with the spirit of consolation and joy; the imprisoned by evil and sin with the spirit of inner freedom; those who hate with the spirit of love; the disappointed with the spirit of hope, the violent with the spirit of meekness; the unjust with the spirit of justice; the unmerciful with the spirit of mercy; those fallen into alcohol and drugs with the spirit of sobriety; the lazy with the spirit of diligence; those who resist Your Will with the spirit of cooperation with You; the miserly with the spirit of generosity; the proud with the spirit of humility; those who have authority in the Church and in the world with the spirit of service; those who kill unborn life with the spirit of life; and those overcome by the spirit of lies with the spirit of truth. Grant that through fasting and prayer all conflicts and wars may be eliminated and Your Kingdom of love and peace, justice and truth may come to all men and nations.

Our Father, 10 Hail Marys, Glory Be, O my Jesus. . .

Fourth Glorious Mystery

I give glory to You, O Father, for having assumed Mary, body and soul, into Heaven. Thank You for having rewarded Her faithfulness to Your Son with a majestic celebration in Heaven. Be blessed in Her fasting and prayers, in Her love and faithfulness. Thank You, Mary, for being close to us through Your apparitions even though You have been assumed into Heaven.

I offer this day of fasting and prayer with You for all those who are faithful to Your message. May they receive the strength to remain faithful in every life situation so as to remain with You their entire lives until their glorious entry into heaven. I especially offer my fasting and prayer for the youth so that in You, O Mary, they may discover the Mother and the Teacher so that they may overcome all of life's difficulties and trials of this world. Through fasting and prayer may they be able to discern evil and its traps and successfully fight against the seduction waiting for them in the world. May all the young recognize the Star of Salvation and Hope in You. May they continue their way with You in faithfulness to Jesus and may they accept Him as their Way, Truth, Light and Life.

Our Father, 10 Hail Marys, Glory Be, O my Jesus. . .

Fifth Glorious Mystery

I give glory to You Father, for having crowned Mary as the Queen of Heaven and Earth and for sending Her to us as the Queen of Peace. Thank You, Mary, for being tireless with us and for praying and interceding for us.

I offer this day of fasting and prayer, to which You call me, for Your intentions so that peace may enter into every heart, into every family, into the Church and into the world. I offer it for the reconciliation of those living in dissension; for the unbelievers to come to experience the love of the Father; for families to start to pray; for the conquering of every evil and of the evil one. I offer it for all of Your intentions in which You call us to participate with You in fasting and prayer. Let it be so.

Our Father, 10 Hail Marys, Glory Be, O my Jesus. . .

Concluding prayer:

On this day of fasting and prayer, I thank You, Heavenly Father, in the name of Your Son Jesus Christ together with Mary, Ever Virgin, for giving me the grace to enter with my entire being into the Mysteries of Their lives. Grant that in this way, I may discover Your immeasurable love with which You love all creatures. Fill all of us, Your children, with the Spirit of fasting and prayer, so that we may be able to recognize and fulfill Your will; to love You above everything else; to love our neighbors as ourselves; and to love and protect all nature as a special expression of Your love towards us. We implore You: may Your peace pour forth into all hearts through the intercession of Mary, in the name of Your Son Jesus Christ, the King of Peace. Let it be so. Amen.

12.3. The Way of the Cross on a Fast Day

PRAYER AT THE GARDEN OF GETHSEMANE

While the Apostles slept, You prayed alone, abandoned. Judas prepared Your betrayal. You were sorrowful unto death. You perspired blood and asked: "My Father let this cup pass from me."

Forgive me, Jesus, for often being spiritually lukewarm and tired. Have mercy on those who suffer and who are now in danger. Have mercy on all those who are in a life and death struggle. Send them Your angel of consolation and the strength to follow You faithfully on the Way of the Cross.

On this day of fasting and prayer grant me, O Lord, the grace that I may follow You on this Way of the Cross as Mary, Your faithful Mother, did.

- Have mercy on us, O Lord.
- Have mercy on us.

Stood the mournful Mother weeping
At the Cross Her station keeping
Seeing Her Son crucified.

Holy Mother hear my prayers,
in my heart, renew each wound
of Jesus my Savior.

FIRST STATION:
JESUS, PILATE CONDEMNES YOU TO DEATH

- We adore You O Christ, and we praise You
- because by Your holy Cross You have redeemed the world.

Pilate knew that You were innocent but nonetheless condemned You. He did not dare to intervene for the just and true solution to free You because he was afraid of losing his authority, power, and prestige: He was afraid of others who were in power and of the people. He had no freedom in his heart and that is why he could not decide for truth and justice with love.

You accepted Your condemnation with love because Your heart was free; because You loved, fasted and prayed.

Today I offer to You all the condemnations I used to condemn and reject others because there was no freedom or love in my heart. I offer to You all the condemnations I received from others as a result of which I, in turn, responded with condemnation, anger, threats and a desire for revenge. On this day of fasting and prayer, I beseech You: free my heart from every slavery to evil and sin and every slavery to power, honor, material things and pleasures. Grant that I may be able to love and forgive.

I offer my fasting to You and I pray for all those in power in the world and for all those responsible in the Church. By the power of fasting and prayer, free them for justice, love, truth and peace. I also offer my fasting and prayer for all those who suffer due to unjust behavior and unjust solutions. Grant that they may be able to accept their condemnation with peace. Heal their hearts and souls so that peace may reign in their hearts and in the hearts of all men.

(In silence now offer to the Lord the person because of whom you suffer and the person who suffers because of you. Pray, forgive and seek the strength for forgiveness.)

Our Father, Hail Mary, Glory Be.

- *Have mercy on us, O Lord.*
- *Have mercy on us.*

Through Her heart, His sorrow sharing,
All His bitter anguish bearing,
Now at length the sword has passed.

Holy Mother hear my prayers,
in my heart, renew each wound
of Jesus my Saviour.

SECOND STATION:
JESUS, YOU RECEIVE YOUR CROSS

- *We adore You O Christ, and we praise You*
- *because by Your holy Cross You have redeemed the world.*

On Your shoulders now is the Cross they decided You were to die on. It injures the wounds You have already received from scourging, but You accept it with love. The words You spoke as the Teacher to Your Disciples You now fulfill to the letter: "Whoever wants to be my disciple, let him take up his cross and follow me." You accepted the Cross in order to teach us how we are to carry our crosses and in order to free us from our crosses. Thank You.

On this day of fasting and prayer, I implore You to give me the interior light so that in humility and freedom of heart I may recognize all situations in which I have rejected the cross. Grant that I may recognize all situations where, with my words and behavior, I have placed crosses on individuals I live and work with – on those near to me. I admit that I am often blind to the sufferings I have caused to others and I only see what others have done to me. Because of this, I am discontent and angry. I complain, gossip and unjustly accuse others. Through fasting and prayer, may my heart become free and cleansed so that I may become Your disciple and that You may be my Teacher.

I offer this fasting and prayer to You for all those who are also blind to their behavior; those who in pride, envy, jealousy and addiction, place heavy crosses on the shoulders of others. They do not see others nor are they concerned about them. They only seek their own rights, pleasures and sinful indulgences. May fasting and prayer cleanse and purify hearts and bring peace and order into interpersonal relationships.

(Now offer to Jesus everyone who has placed crosses of suffering on Your shoulders and pray that you may recognize all those you have placed crosses of suffering upon. Forgive. Seek the strength for forgiveness.)

Our Father, Hail Mary, Glory Be.
- *Have mercy on us, O Lord.*
- *Have mercy on us.*

Oh how sad and sore distressed
Was that Mother highly blest
Of the sole-begotten Son.

Holy Mother hear my prayers,
in my heart, renew each wound
of Jesus my Savior.

THIRD STATION:

JESUS, YOU FALL THE FIRST TIME BENEATH THE CROSS

- We adore You O Christ, and we praise You
- because by Your holy Cross You have redeemed the world.

I am grateful to You, Jesus, because I know that You accepted the Cross willingly and with love, even though You were so physically weakened that You fell under It. You did not get angry with those who placed the Cross on Your shoulders nor did You complain because of Your fall. Instead, You offered this moment with love for us: so that we may be able to get up when we fall; so that we may not remain under our crosses when they cause us to fall to the ground; and so that we may not condemn those who rejoice in our fall. Thank You.

On this day of fasting and prayer, give me the grace to become conscious of my falls and of my behavior when I fall.

Give me the grace to understand that I have so often and easily fallen because I have not fasted or prayed enough. In this way, I remained without inner strength. Grant that again today I can decide for fasting and prayer.

I offer to You all of the situations in which I have fallen and lost love, faith, hope, peace, patience, goodness and mercy. I offer to You the consequences of such falls in my heart, which prevented me from getting up and following You. I offer to You all those whom I have condemned when I have fallen. I also offer to You all of the bitterness accumulated in my heart against them. Grant, O Lord, that by the power of fasting and prayer, I can get up and follow You.

I offer my fasting and prayer to You for all those who have fallen because I was not strong and for those whom I caused to fall because of my own evil and sinfulness. Grant them the grace to get up and to forgive me, so that in peace and togetherness, we may carry each other's burdens. Grant that we may get up after falling and continue our way with You.

(Offer your own situation to the Lord: your falls, all those because of whom you have fallen and those who have caused you to fall. Also, with gratitude, offer all those who have helped you get up again and those you helped to get up.)

Our Father, Hail Mary, Glory Be.
- *Have mercy on us, O Lord.*
- *Have mercy on us.*

Is there one who would not weep,
Whelmed in miseries so deep
Christ's dear Mother to behold?

Holy Mother hear my prayers,
in my heart, renew each wound
of Jesus my Savior.

FOURTH STATION:
JESUS, YOU MEET YOUR HOLY MOTHER

- We adore You O Christ, and we praise You
- because by Your holy Cross You have redeemed the world.

Jesus and Mary - Son and Mother - You met on the way of the Cross. Your pure, good and humble hearts that were never tainted by evil, sin, pride or selfishness were moved even more by suffering and affliction. Your meeting was full of love, hope, faith, understanding and compassion. In Your meeting the walk with the Cross was not stopped nor was the death sentence lifted. Nonetheless it was a meeting of consolation and encouragement. It was a surrender to the Will of the Father anew and a readiness to fulfill His Will completely. Thank You, Jesus, for Your meeting with Mary. Thank You, Mary, for Your meeting with Jesus.

On this day of fasting and prayer, I reflect on my own meetings in my family: with my parents, brothers and sisters, children, husband, wife, daughter-in-law, sister-in-law and others. I thank You for all the beautiful and good meetings and offer to You all those meetings in which others burdened me and I burdened others. I offer my fasting and prayer for the healing of the wounds which came about because of our pride, selfishness, impatience, lack of forgiveness, lack of love and lack of openness to each other. Through fasting and prayer may our hearts become free for love and forgiveness, mercy and understanding, obedience and respect. I offer my fasting and prayer for all those whose hearts have sunk into material things and are imprisoned by alcohol, drugs, unbelief and disobedience. May peace enter into all families.

(Now in silence, offer to the Lord your parents and other members of your family; give thanks, pray, forgive and seek the strength for forgiveness.)

Our Father, Hail Mary, Glory Be.

- Have mercy on us, O Lord.
- Have mercy on us.

Oh how sad and sore distressed
Was that Mother highly blest
Of the sole-begotten Son.

Holy Mother hear my prayers,
in my heart, renew each wound
of Jesus my Savior.

FIFTH STATION:
JESUS, SIMON THE CYRENE HELPS YOU CARRY YOUR CROSS

- We adore You O Christ, and we praise You
- because by Your holy Cross You have redeemed the world.

Jesus, with gratitude, You handed Your Cross to Simon who carried it for a while. How lovely it is when there is someone who is prepared to help carry the Cross! You came to help everyone and now You accept help from Simon. Thank You, Jesus. Thank you Simon, for your good deed to my Savior.

Today, Jesus, I offer to You my fasting and prayer so that You may purify my heart from selfishness, pride, avarice, greed and everything that hinders me from being prepared to carry the crosses of others. Free me from what hinders me from permitting others to help me.

Heal the wounds in the hearts of those who expected help from me when I failed to notice them, because I was imprisoned by my own selfishness, by material things, by a rush for pleasure and an easy life -- without a willingness to sacrifice. I fast and pray that all those who are wealthy may help the poor; that all the healthy may help the sick; and that all the young may accept the elderly. By fasting and prayer, purify my heart and the hearts of all men, so that we may all be sensitive to

155

the needs of others and resolute in helping them. Be blessed in all those who have helped me up to now and in those whom I was able to help.

(In silence, offer to the Lord all those whom you know are now wounded because of a lack of readiness to have you help them. Make concrete decisions and pray that you may be able carry them out.)

Our Father, Hail Mary, Glory Be.

- *Have mercy on us, O Lord.*
- *Have mercy on us.*

Who could see that Mother's grief
without being saddened too,
While She suffers with Her Son?

Holy Mother hear my prayers,
in my heart, renew each wound
of Jesus my Savior.

SIXTH STATION:
JESUS, VERONICA OFFERS YOU HER VEIL AND WIPES YOUR FACE

- *We adore You O Christ, and we praise You*
- *because by Your holy Cross You have redeemed the world.*

Your divine face was covered in blood. It was spat upon. People deformed it. They humiliated You because their own evil and sin imprisoned them. Veronica overcame every fear and all regard as she wiped Your face. Out of gratitude, You gave her an imprint of Your image. Thank You, Jesus.

Jesus, today I offer my fasting and prayer to You to cleanse me from every evil and every bad habit; so that my face may shine with joy and peace, love and hope. Grant that Your face may be recognized in mine; that Your Word may be recognized in my words and that Your peace may be recognized as my peace. Through fasting and prayer may the lines on my face that came about because my heart was not free; the lines that came about when my face expressed bitterness, anger, hatred, tension, agitation, nervousness, aggression, dissatisfaction, the insatiable appetite for food and drink and the desire of pleasure fade away. Through fasting and prayer may serenity, love and mercy enter into every heart. May peace come to all.

Today I offer my fasting and prayer for all those who swear and curse God. Fill their hearts with good and gentle words. Fill them with prayer and Your gratitude.

I offer this fasting and prayer for the grace of a good Confession, so that every meeting in Confession may be a meeting with You. Grant that all of us can come to shine with a new radiance that comes from You. I also pray to You for confessors so that they may be an extended hand of Your mercy.

(In silence, offer to the Lord everything by which you wounded yourself or you continue to wound yourself with. Offer to Him all those who, by their behavior, wound the faces of others forgetting that each face is always the face of Jesus.)

Our Father, Hail Mary, Glory Be.
- *Have mercy on us, O Lord.*
- *Have mercy on us.*

For the sins of all the people
Saw Jesus hang in desolation,
All with bloody scourges rent.

Holy Mother hear my prayers,
in my heart, renew each wound
of Jesus my Savior.

SEVENTH STATION:
JESUS, YOU FALL THE SECOND TIME BENEATH THE CROSS

- We adore You O Christ, and we praise You
- because by Your holy Cross You have redeemed the world.

The second fall was harder than the first. Your physical strength was at its end. You were tired. It was even more difficult to get up again to continue Your walk with the cross. Nonetheless, You rose by the power of Your will and love which inspired You to sacrifice everything for us; as the Lamb of God, as the Servant of God, who heals and saves us with His wounds. You had the strength to get up because You fasted and prayed. Thank You.

I offer this day of fasting and prayer to You to overcome all my weaknesses and faults so that You may forgive me for my repeated falls, my unfaithfulness to the promises not to fall again and for all my physical, mental and spiritual fatigue. Give me the strength to get up and to follow You.

I offer to You all those who have fallen again and have lost faith, love, hope, trust and the will to get up again. By the power of fasting and prayer, help them to receive Your help with an open heart so as to get up and follow You, their Lord, with a new strength and a new determination.

I especially offer this day of fasting and prayer to You for all those who, in their torment and difficulty, are in danger today of deciding against a conceived life and are tempted to kill the child. By the power of fasting and prayer, give them the light of faith to come to love the unborn life and to decide for it. By the power of fasting and prayer, grant the grace of repentance and conversion and the grace to serve life from now on, to all those who have committed crime against unborn children. I offer this day of fasting and prayer to You for all pregnant mothers, for fathers of unborn children, for their families, for the doctors and for all those who advise pregnant mothers in their difficulties – may they respect and protect life.

(Offer your personal situation to the Lord and offer to Him all those you know are fatigued or have killed an innocent child. Pray for them.)

Our Father, Hail Mary, Glory Be.
- *Have mercy on us, O Lord.*
- *Have mercy on us.*

See this most beloved Son,
dying there in desolation
Till His Spirit, forth He sent.

Holy Mother hear my prayers,
in my heart, renew each wound
of Jesus my Savior.

EIGHTH STATION:
JESUS, YOU CONSOLE THE WOMEN OF JERUSALEM

- *We adore You O Christ, and we praise You*
- *because by Your holy Cross You have redeemed the world.*

Jesus, You did not permit the women of Jerusalem to cry over Your destiny. Instead You stopped and called them to conversion so that, through conversion, they could save themselves, their families and their people. At every opportunity, You proclaimed the Good News about the Father's Kingdom. This is why You did not neglect this opportunity to speak to the women who were crying for You.

I offer this day of fasting and prayer to You for myself. Grant that I may always listen to Your Word and accept It in the freedom of heart and soul. Through fasting and prayer, may I be purified from everything that makes me blind to the signs of Your love and deaf to Your Word. Today I fast and pray for all those for whom Your Word is intended - for all Christians - so that free from every slavery to the world and sin, in the depth of their hearts, they can all recognize Your signs of love and hear Your Word.

I offer this day of fasting and prayer to You for the Pope, for all Bishops, priests, missionaries and teachers of faith. By fasting and prayer may they first become listeners of the Word and then proclaim It to others. May Your Spirit inspire and lead them so that, in the power of Your Spirit, they may proclaim Your Word. May signs and wonders accompany them just as wondrous signs of Your power and might accompanied the proclamation of Your Word by the Apostles and so many Saints in the Church.

I especially offer this fasting and prayer to You for every priest consciously to accept his assignment of proclamation, forgiveness of sins, the healing of the sick and deliverance from evil spirits. May Your Kingdom of freedom, peace, justice and life come to all people and nations. I fast and pray to You for new vocations in the Church; for the young to respond to, and accept Your call.

(Offer to the Lord all those situations in which you have listened to God's Word without desire and joy. Offer to Him all obstacles you feel are causing you to be blind and deaf to what He has given you or wanted to give to you but you did not receive because you did not fast and pray sufficiently. With faith, offer your fasting and prayer for all those who need them the most at this moment.)

Our Father, Hail Mary, Glory Be.

- *Have mercy on us, O Lord.*
- *Have mercy on us.*

May the flame of my own heart,
Love Jesus Your Son,

So that I please Him.

Holy Mother hear my prayers,
in my heart, renew each wound
of Jesus my Savior.

NINTH STATION:
JESUS, YOU FALL THE THIRD TIME BENEATH THE CROSS

- We adore You O Christ, and we praise You
- because by Your holy Cross You have redeemed the world.

Jesus, You fell the third time beneath the Cross. I do not even dare contemplate what it was like for You at this moment. You were completely exhausted, tired and humiliated. You lay beneath Your Cross and with Your final strength, You got up and continued on. Your knees buckled and trembled. Your wounds were injured once again. Your entire body was in total agony. Only Your love for us was stronger; it gave You the strength to get up and to continue on. Also at this fall, You repeated in Your heart what You said in the Garden of Gethsemane, "Father may Your Will be done." My Jesus, thank You.

I offer this fasting and prayer to You for all those who have lost their inner freedom in alcohol, drugs, gambling, immorality, prostitution and other bad habits. Today I offer this day of fasting and prayer to You for all of them. They have completely destroyed their human dignity, their spiritual, mental and physical health and have become slaves to their bad habits. Those who live with them suffer much. By the power of fasting and prayer, illuminate their hearts with a deep desire for liberation and send them someone to help them. Give them the strength to conquer evil and to get up and follow You. Grant that they may not be afraid of sacrifice and renunciation so that they may again obtain faith, love, hope and trust. May joy and peace return into their hearts. Give them the strength to forgive themselves and to forgive those they blame for their falls. May they become witnesses of the strength that comes from You. I offer this fasting and prayer to You for all those who have absolutely no will to get up again and will not admit that they need help. Illuminate their darkened reason, strengthen their weakened and broken will and free them from negative influences so that all people can live in peace.

(In silence, offer to the Lord everything that is not good in your heart and in your behavior. Offer to Him all those you know who are in bad situations. Pray for them.)

Our Father, Hail Mary, Glory Be.

- *Have mercy on us, O Lord.*
- *Have mercy on us.*

Thy Son in torment on the Cross,
Who for me was crucified
Let me share with Thee His pain.

Holy Mother hear my prayers,
in my heart, renew each wound
of Jesus my Savior.

TENTH STATION:
JESUS, YOU ARE STRIPPED OF YOUR GARMENTS

- *We adore You O Christ, and we praise You*
- *because by Your holy Cross You have redeemed the world.*

Jesus, in carrying Your Cross, You came to the place You decided to give Your life for us on the Cross. Before the actual Crucifixion, yet another thing occurred to Your tormentors: to strip You of Your garments. They exposed You, naked, before the eyes of men with more ridicule and abasing words. You endured everything patiently and with love in order to redeem us from all of our humiliations and sins against human dignity. A question comes to me at this station, "Did You have to

162

suffer all of this and take it upon Yourself?" An answer is imparted, ´Yes´, You had to, because my sins and the sins of the world are great. You decided to free us from condemnation that has befallen us because of our sins. Thank You Jesus.

I offer this day of fasting and prayer to You in thanksgiving for Your immeasurable love. I also offer to You all that I have done to humiliate myself personally: all the sins of the body that I have committed and all the sins of the world by which man is humiliated.

I offer this day of fasting and prayer to You for all those who, as children, have experienced humiliation, rejection and sexual violence from their families and those nearest to them. I also offer to You all those who have sinned against the dignity of unborn life; all political prisoners, all those who have been stripped of their freedom because of their evil doings and crimes; and for all those who use their positions of power and money to abuse and humiliate others. By Your suffering and humiliation, free every heart and return human dignity to all.

(Now offer all of your sins of the body to the Lord. Pray for forgiveness and conversion for all those you know are in situations of destroying their human dignity and the dignity of others at this time.)

Our Father, Hail Mary, Glory Be.
- *Have mercy on us, O Lord.*
- *Have mercy on us.*

Let me mingle tears with thee,
For Jesus dear, beloved,
All the days that I may live.

Holy Mother hear my prayers,
in my heart, renew each wound
of Jesus my Savior.

ELEVENTH STATION:
JESUS, YOU ARE BEING NAILED TO THE CROSS

- We adore You O Christ, and we praise You
- because by Your holy Cross You have redeemed the world.

The end of Your Passion is drawing near, yet the most difficult moments still lie ahead. You were condemned to a death on the Cross and Your Crucifixion followed. No heart will ever be able to sense all the pain You suffered when the soldiers, using sharp nails, hammered Your hands and feet to the wood of the Cross. Even this horrendous moment You offered with love for us and for the entire world, so that, by the power of Your suffering, the Father could free the world from violence and killing. In this way, You identified Yourself with all the victims of violence and murder in this world. You also used this most difficult moment to offer once again, Your life for us with love. Thank You my Jesus, my Crucified Savior.

I offer this day of fasting and prayer to You for all those who, to attain position, power and money, are ruthless and commit violence by abusing and crucifying others to suffer on various crosses. I offer this day to You for those who are experiencing bitterness and hatred; for those who are prepared for revenge, to repay evil with evil. I fast and pray for all those who are violent that they may recognize their sin and sinful behavior; for all those who have provoked and caused conflicts in families, in the Church and in the world, by their behavior; for all those who instigate wars and destruction; and for all those who violate children, the sick, the poor, the innocent and the helpless. Give them the grace to admit all of their acts of violence. May they turn to You, the God of peace, love and forgiveness and become peacemakers.

I offer this day of fasting and prayer for all the victims of family violence and for all the victims of violence in the Church and in the world. May they all forgive and be healed. May they be able to extend their hand of reconciliation to all those who have, in any way, inflicted evil upon them.

May the blows of hatred, envy, jealousy, and ill will, by which we easily nail others to the cross, stop.

Jesus, by the power of Your Spirit of meekness and peace, stop all types of violence so that Your Kingdom of love and peace can come to all mankind.

Stop every initiation and step towards war. May wars disappear and may Your Kingdom come to all. I offer this fasting and prayer for all those who are tempted to commit violence against their own life or against the lives of others. Enable them to serve You, the One and the Only, the Good, the Just, and the True, with love; with all their hearts and souls.

(In silence, offer to the Lord the violence others have committed against you and the violence you have committed against others. Pray and ask for forgiveness so that peace may come to dwell in every heart.)

Our Father, Hail Mary, Glory Be.
- *Have mercy on us, O Lord.*
- *Have mercy on us.*

Virgin of all virgins blest!
Listen to my fond request:
Let me share Thy grief divine.

Holy Mother hear my prayers,
in my heart, renew each wound
of Jesus my Savior.

TWELFTH STATION:
JESUS, YOU ARE DYING ON THE CROSS

- *We adore You O Christ, and we praise You*
- *because by Your holy Cross You have redeemed the world.*

Jesus, Lamb of God, You hung crucified upon the Cross. Reveal to me Your love that brought You to this moment; this love by which You gave Your life for my Salvation in this way – so that I, too, may respond with love and that Your love may be loved. First of all, I ask You, my dying Lord, for love – because without love, I cannot enter into Your Passion and Death.

May my heart, my soul, and my entire being be moved by this sight: the Son of God is crucified for me between two criminals -- He bleeds, He suffers, He is ridiculed, He is insulted and He is completely humiliated. At the end of His strength, suffocating, He pronounces words of prayer invoking the Father -- He prays for forgiveness, He gives His Mother to the disciple, and the disciple, to the Mother. With a mighty cry to the Father, He dies.

(Stop for a moment. Be still and remain in silence. In the face of great events, words are helpless. Have compassion and remain with Mary who prayed and experienced and followed all of this with Her Motherly love.)

My dead Savior, I offer this day of fasting and love to You. Grant that Your love may open my eyes so that I may be able to see and open my ears, so that I may be able to hear everything that has taken place at this moment. May Your pain, Your prayer and Your words of forgiveness now resound in my heart and change my life. May everything in me that stands in the way of complete surrender to the will of the Father, die. I renounce every sin and evil. Through Your sacrifice, by the power of fasting and prayer, I ask You to free me so that I may be able to offer myself, together with You, for my own salvation and the salvation of the world.

Grant inner strength to all those who are now crucified, because they have given themselves over to the forces of evil. May they be freed. Grant strength to all those who are crucified by others who are unjust, avaricious, and voracious for power and honor; by those who hate and crucify everyone around them with their violence. May evil die, and goodness rise; may all lack of peace die, and peace be born; may hopelessness die, and hope be born. May everything turn to good.

(In silence, offer to the Lord everything in you that you know must be gone from your words and behavior. Offer to Him all those whom you have crucified and all those who have crucified you. Pray for the strength to forgive. Pray for all those who are dying and for all those who are not able to forgive others. Pray for those who have intentionally or unintentionally killed someone. Pray for those who have killed unborn children or have participated in killing.)

Our Father, Hail Mary, Glory Be.
- *Have mercy on us, O Lord.*
- *Have mercy on us.*

Let me be wounded with His wounds
Be saturated with His Cross,
And with the blood of Your dear Son.

Holy Mother hear my prayers,
in my heart, renew each wound
of Jesus my Savior.

THIRTEENTH STATION:
JESUS, YOU ARE TAKEN DOWN FROM THE CROSS AND PLACED IN THE EMBRACE OF YOUR MOTHER

- *We adore You O Christ, and we praise You*
- *because by Your holy Cross You have redeemed the world.*

O Mary, Sorrowful Mother, when at the Annunciation, You said to God, "Let it be done to Me according to Your Word." You did not realize what Your consent encompassed. At this moment, in the depth of Your sorrow, You again repeated in Your heart, "Father, let it be done to Me according to Your Word." Who could ever comprehend the pain of Your Motherly heart as You helplessly watched the Passion and the Crucifixion; as You watched Your Crucified Son hanging on the Cross and as You witnessed His Death? Mary, You experienced all of this. You suffered and loved. You prayed with Him.

167

You forgave when Jesus forgave and You also asked the Father to forgive them. Thank You, Mary, for Your love and suffering with Your Son Jesus for us. In Your pain, You became our Mother. Through this experience of pain and suffering, You became the Mother and Consoler to all those who suffer. You became 'Comforter of the Afflicted' and hope to all those who have lost hope. You learned how to suffer and You understand our affliction. Thank You.

In trying to live Your messages, I offer this day of fasting and prayer for myself that I may be freed from everything hindering me from completely consecrating myself to You - so that I may be completely Yours. I consecrate my past, my present and my future to You to help me remain faithful. I consecrate to You all families, parents with children, all widows, all orphans, all youth, the entire Church and the world.

I offer this fasting and prayer for Your intentions and for the Triumph of Your Immaculate Heart.

(In silence speak to Our Lady about yourself and tell Her your plans, difficulties, disappointments and problems. Converse with Her as you should with a mother.)

Our Father, Hail Mary, Glory Be.

- *Have mercy on us, O Lord.*
- *Have mercy on us.*

Be to me, O Virgin, nigh,
Lest in flames I burn and die.
In His awful Judgment day.

Holy Mother hear my prayers,
in my heart, renew each wound
of Jesus my Savior.

FOURTEENTH STATION:
JESUS, YOU ARE PLACED INTO THE TOMB

- *We adore You O Christ, and we praise You*
- *because by Your holy Cross You have redeemed the world.*

Mary, You remained almost alone on Calvary. A few of Your most faithful friends were with You sharing Your pain. They helped You place Your Son into the tomb offered by a friend. As He was carried to the tomb, You must have recalled everything He said and did; all of His goodness and love. This is why, at this moment, Your heart was even more sorrowful. You must have wondered how people could be like this, but disappointment did not enter into Your soul. Thank You for Your love that was stronger than the attack of hatred. Thank You for Your faith that was stronger than lack of trust in God Who permitted all of this. Thank You for Your hope, which did not extinguish when the stone sealed the tomb, finally separating Your Son from the light of day and the light of the living.

Together with You, I once again want to say thank You to Your Son for coming to this toil-worn earth; for the time He dwelt among us sinners and for everything that others failed to thank Him for.

I offer this day of fasting and prayer to be able to discover and fulfill the Will of the Father in everything; so that in the end, I can peacefully accept death and wait for a new life. I also offer this fasting and prayer for all those who have strayed from the true way; for those who walk the ways of evil and do not think of their end; for all those who do not believe in victory over death and see an end to life at the moment of death; and for all those who do not believe in eternal life and do not prepare themselves with seriousness for the moment of their passing from this world.

(Consecrate the moment of your death to Jesus through Mary. Pray for a happy and meritorious death and for all those who will be with you at the moment of your death. Pray for the dying.)

Our Father, Hail Mary, Glory Be.
- *Have mercy on us, O Lord.*
- *Have mercy on us.*

While my body here decays,
May my soul Thy goodness praise,
With Your glory forever!

Holy Mother hear my prayers,
in my heart, renew each wound
of Jesus my Savior.

12.4. PRAYER BEFORE THE CROSS

The parish priest, Fr. Bernardin Smoljan and the parishioners completed this 8.5 meter Cross of reinforced concrete on March 15, 1934. On the Cross, they inscribed the words:

"TO JESUS CHRIST, THE REDEEMER OF THE HUMAN RACE, AS A SIGN OF OUR FAITH, LOVE AND HOPE, IN MEMORY OF THE 1900 ANNIVERSARY OF THE PASSION OF JESUS."

A relic of the true Cross, honored by Christians as a part of the Cross on which Jesus was crucified, was received from Rome and built into this Cross. This relic was obtained from the larger part of the true Cross which remains in the Church of 'Santa Croce di Gerusalemme' in Rome. Ever since the Cross was erected, in honor of the Triumph of the Cross, Holy Mass has been celebrated on the first Sunday following the feast of the Birth of the Blessed Virgin Mary on September 8th.

We adore Your most Holy Cross, Lord Jesus, for it is the sign of Your love. Through the power of Your most precious blood, cleanse us from all our sins and protect us from every Satanic influence. May a river of peace and reconciliation flow from this place into the Parish community, the Church and the entire world. Bless and call into heaven all those who have built this Cross. Bless all those who have prayed before it and those who will pray before it, for they have listened to Mary, Your Mother. It is She who calls us to pray before the Cross and teaches us that great graces come from the Cross. Be blessed, O Lord Jesus, for by Your Holy Cross You have redeemed us for eternal life.

Once again, I offer to You my fasting and prayer for my own salvation and the salvation of all people. Amen.

(Pray 5 Our Fathers in honor of the 5 wounds of Jesus.)

On your descent from Cross Mountain, you will see the station depicting the Resurrection. Pause for a moment and pray. Sing an appropriate song honoring Jesus' Resurrection before you descend in silence. If you pray the Way of the Cross at home or in your parish church, you should likewise remember His Resurrection.

12.5. Eucharistic Adoration on a Fast Day

Mary calls us to a life with bread and water and the deepest meaning of this life with bread and water is in preparation for a meeting with Jesus in the Eucharist. While the foremost meeting with Jesus should take place in Holy Communion during Holy Mass, in Mary's school, Adoration is a very important time of meeting with Him. In Her messages, Our Lady has spoken about Adoration:

"Tonight also, dear children, I am grateful to you in a special way for being here. Unceasingly adore the Most Blessed Sacrament of the Altar. I am always present when the faithful are adoring. Special graces are then being received." (March 15, 1984)

"Dear children! Today I invite you to fall in love with the Most Holy Sacrament of the Altar. Adore Him, little children, in your Parishes and in this way you will be united with the entire world. Jesus will become your friend and you will not talk of Him like someone whom you barely know. Union with Him will be a joy for you and you will become witnesses to the love of Jesus that He has for every creature. Little children, when you adore Jesus you are also close to me. Thank you for having responded to my call." (September 25, 1995)

Jesus spoke about bread and, in the end, took the bread and said, "This is My Body which will be given up for you." He took the chalice and said, "This is the cup of My Blood, . . .it will be shed for you and for all men."

Everything He said about bread, including the multiplication of loaves, was in preparation for the Eucharist. Mary wants nothing else than to bring us to the Heavenly Bread by our life with bread. That is why Adoration on a fast day is a very important part of the weekly program of fasting and those who fast, adore day and night. Experiences of those who fast confirm the importance of spending time with Jesus alone in Adoration at night.

(To begin with, if possible, a Eucharistic song is sung to calm us and to lead us into Adoration. . .)

Jesus I adore You. I believe that You are True God and True man hidden in this Consecrated Host because You said, "this is My Body given up for You." Today on this day of fasting and prayer, my day of life with bread, I want to adore You, the Heavenly Bread. I ask You to remove from me everything that still hinders me from meeting You in this Host; from meeting You, the Living and True God, Emmanuel - God, Who decided to remain with us in this simple way. At this moment, I have decided to be with You. Quiet my thoughts and feelings and direct my desires to You. Grant that I may be completely still before You.

(Remain in silence for a while)

(If there are sufficient people, a refrain can be sung following each period of silence.)

I adore You, Jesus, the Bread of Life, and I thank You for the words, "I am the Bread of Life, whoever comes to me will never hunger, and whoever believes in me will never thirst. . . .I am the Bread that came down from Heaven. . . I am the Bread of Life . . ." (cf. Jn 6,35-48) Jesus, on this day of my life with bread, I implore You: open my heart and grant that I may comprehend Your love, which You show us by becoming our Bread. Awaken a deep hunger in me for You, the Bread of Life. Awaken hunger in me for Your Word and Your love.

(Remain in silence and continue to converse with Jesus in your own words.)

I adore You, Jesus, the Living Bread, and the Bread from Heaven. I adore You for my life and the life of the world. I thank You because You are so in love with me that You became the Bread for my life. Mary, Your Mother, calls me to fall in love with You. Today, as I live with bread, give me the grace to have my heart fall completely in love with You. Grant that from now on, You may be foremost in my thoughts, my words and in each of my actions. Give me the grace to meet others as someone who is in love with You. Then it will not be difficult for me to forgive, to love and to be merciful. I especially implore You: grant me the grace to accept the way of bread without any fear, so that like You, I can say, "this is my body for you." Grant that I may be able to say in my family, in my community, to my people and to everyone who is in need, "Here I am on the table of life for you as good bread, love, hope, mercy and forgiveness. Take me and you will experience God's love, mercy, forgiveness and goodness."

(Remain in silence and pray, permit the love of Jesus to embrace you. . .)

I adore You, Jesus, the living Bread, and I thank You for having accepted the way of the 'grain' - for having accepted to die. Thank You for the new life born from Your death. I now offer to You all of the 'weeds' that have crept into my life, my thoughts, my plans, my words and my actions. I offer to You my pride, selfishness, envy, jealousy, attachment to material things and all of my bad habits that do not permit me to become bread for the life of others. I offer to You everything that makes my life bitter, agonizing and indigestible for others. Thank You for granting me the power of Your Spirit that I may be free to love as You do.

(Remain in silence and offer to Jesus everything that you find in your life that is not according to God's will.

Offer to Him everything that hinders you from becoming bread for others.)

I adore You, Jesus and I thank You for not having given in to Satan when You fasted in the desert. While You fasted, Satan came to You and said, "If You are truly the Son of God, command that these stones become loaves of bread." Jesus, You said in reply, "It is written, one does not live by bread alone, but by every Word that comes forth from the mouth of God." (Mt 4,3-4)

I offer to You this day of a life with bread in prayer to free my heart from every greed and every addiction to material things. Free my heart from disproportionate eating and drinking so that, in the freedom of my heart, in each situation, I may comprehend that I do not only live on bread and material things. Grant that I may resist temptation and can begin to live on, and be nurtured by, the Word of God.

I offer to You this day of a life with bread in prayer also for all those who have forgotten that Your Word is as necessary for life as food is. I offer it for those who have permitted greed and covetousness to rule over their hearts; those continually provoking conflict and causing disorder; those behaving unjustly and obtaining material goods unfairly.

I offer this day of a life with bread in prayer for all those who are rich and have given their lives completely over to material things: to pleasures, debauchery, unrestraint and extravagance. They take advantage of those who work for them and refuse to share with their poor brothers. Grant that each one of us may say, "I do not live on bread alone. I also need the Word of God." Grant that we may live in this way.

(In silence, offer to Lord all of your addictions and everything that causes you anguished concern. Offer to Him all of insatiability among people and pray.)

I adore You, Jesus, the Living Bread, and I thank You, because in Your fasting and prayer in the desert, You have shown Your complete obedience to Your Father. You refused to put Him to the test. Satan, the tempter, led You to the Holy city, placed You on the parapet of the temple and said, "If You are the Son of God, throw Yourself down. For it is written, He will command His angels concerning You and 'with their hands they will support You, lest You dash Your foot against a stone.' " Thank You for Your answer, "It is also written, 'You shall not put the Lord, Your God, to the test.' " (Mt 4,5-6)

I offer this day of a life with bread in prayer to You in reparation for all of the situations in my life in which I did not surrender to the Will of the Father; when my pride, selfishness, resistance and fear of His Will led me on the wrong paths – when I followed Satan's incitement and tested the Father. May the Spirit of complete surrender and obedience enter into my heart today so that I may always immediately recognize Satan's deceptions and overcome and chase them away by the power of Your Spirit.

Surrendering to the Will of the Father, I offer to You, Jesus, all those who have reached the pinnacles of their pride, selfishness and godlessness; those who despise You and everyone around them. I also offer to You all those who have descended to the depths of human evil and sin; those who are destroying themselves and living a life unworthy of man, a child of God. Give them the strength not to test the Lord of Lords, but to serve Him devoutly.

(Again pause in silence and tell Jesus about your personal situation. Abandon your heart to Him and offer to Him all those around you. Pray for them.)

I adore You, Jesus and I thank You for having loved the Father so much as to abandon Yourself to Him. You confirmed this abandonment in Your response to the third temptation of Satan, the tempter, during Your fasting and prayer in the desert. Taking You to a very high mountain and showing You all the kingdoms of the world in their magnificence he said to You, "All these I shall give to you, if you prostrate Yourself and worship me." Thank You for your disposition and Your answer, "Be gone, Satan! 'It is written, The Lord Your God, shall you worship and Him alone shall you serve.' " (Mt 4,8-10)

I offer to You this day of a life with bread in prayer for You to purify my heart, so that, together with the Father, in the Holy Spirit, You may occupy the first place in my heart. Today I decide completely for You, together with the Father in the Holy Spirit. I renounce all false gods that I have ever adored and I renounce all things to which I have often resigned my heart. You are my God and Master. I renounce everything of this world and, in Your name, I say to Satan, in Your words, "Be gone, Satan from my thoughts, feelings, decisions and behavior. In the name of Jesus, my Lord, to whom I now give the first place in my life, I renounce you Satan and all your works and all of your deceptions. With all my heart, I want to love the Lord and to adore Him alone."

(Remain in silence in the Lord. In The Name Of Jesus, concretely renounce everything that is now in the first place in your thoughts, words and actions instead of Him.)

Jesus, I also offer my family to You (name each member of your family.) By the power of fasting and prayer, give them the strength to renounce Satan and all his works, so that, in freedom of heart, they can love You and fully serve You.

I offer to You, Jesus, all those responsible in the Church and in the world; all those who have come to worship the authority of this world and its extravagance and wealth. I offer to You all those who have chosen Satan and adore and serve him; all those who are obsessed by Satan; those who are involved in occult and spiritism; all Freemasons and all Satanic sects. Jesus, You are the Lord. By the power and authority given to You by the Father, cast out Satan and free each individual from his influence; free the Church, the world and all nature of him. Grant that all may submit to the Father through You, in the Holy Spirit. Grant that every generation may worship the Father through You, in the Holy Spirit, and that every tongue may joyfully proclaim, "Glory to You, Lord Jesus Christ, the Son of God, in the Holy Spirit!"

(Remain in silence and, in a concrete way, pray for everyone you know; for all the Heads of the Church, for all politicians and for all those who hold positions of responsibility.)

Prayer for blessing:

Jesus, truly alive in this Host, I thank You for Your Presence. Bless me and secure me on the way of peace. Grant me the grace to live from You, the Bread of Life, so that I myself may become a bread of goodness, love and mercy for others. Thank You for Your love for the sick and disabled. Heal my soul and my body. Heal all the sick and helpless. Especially, on this day of a life with bread, I ask You for a spiritual healing for all people: heal our faith, love and hope. Be in the first place in each heart!

Jesus, bless all families, communities, the Church and the world so that, together, we may become a people who not only live from the material bread but from each Word that comes from Your mouth. Free the world from Satan and his works that we may live in peace. Let it be so! Amen.

XIII. CHANGING THE DIET BY FASTING

13.1. Interview with Joseph Sprčić

Joško, as everyone calls him, is a professional masseur and a nutritional expert, specializing with athletes. He completed his studies in China and works in Metković. I asked him for this interview.

Tell me something about healthy nutrition...What does a man need daily to live?

JS: I think that the whole philosophy of living is based on that of lessening the stress on the brain. Current theories on nutrition differ. One is in favor of adding vitamins and the other, promotes fasting. It has been proven that it is better to fast, because with fasting the fatigue on the brain is lessened. How?

Everybody knows from experience that when one eats heavy foods, he sleeps. If one eats frugally, he is in a much better condition. Of the five and a half liters of blood, normally contained in an average, healthy human being, the stomach uses one liter. If the stomach (which is both the furnace of a human being and the organ that warms) is sick, it uses two liters. If a person has an ulcer, gastritis, or stomach ailments, he uses two times as much blood so that is how much less blood and oxygen arrive to the brain. This means that the core operations within a human being simply have neither sufficient circulation nor vitality.

You are involved with sports and with top athletes. What are your experiences?

JS: It is true. I have spent 30 years in sports and with top athletes. Fasting is necessary for athletes, in that it improves their condition and wellbeing. I also recommend fasting for all those who study because

179

immediately after eating, they can study and not get so tired. Those who do not give up heavy foods, lose their concentration and condition. They are distracted or become sleepy. People often think that they will have greater strength from eating hearty foods.

We asked, "Where does this problem begin?" Their eyes were opened to the nature of their injuries and then they understood why it was so easy to be injured. Mucus, located in the stomach (in addition to the food), is utilized for the lubrication of the organs. If the stomach mucus is freed up for the lubrication of the bones and the organs, then there will be no resistance and the muscles won't tear. When heavy foods are consumed, the stomach mucus is not available for the rest of the body because it is being used within the stomach itself.

From your experience: What would be the best nutrition to eat in the morning to sustain oneself until evening?

I would divide that into three categories: food for the sick, food for the healthy and food for athletes. One Chinese proverb says: If a man is sick, he would need seven days to eat grains. When he improves a little, he would need to take 90% grains and 10% other foods; when he is entirely healthy, then he would need to take 50% grains and 50% other foods (milk, meat, etc,.) I was in Singapore in a Catholic convent, which is where I learned much. They are exposed to all other religions and because of this, also gained knowledge from them.

In which form does one eat grains?

There are two standing theories. Eastern theories speak in favor of wheat macrobiotics, (although we identify that the whole grain has benefits) which is the covering layer of the grain and also the wheat germ itself. On this covering are all minerals, and in the wheat germ, is life. Inside part of the grain is the 'whiteness' which bread is made from: gluten and gliadin, which is a starch. This starch is not considered a food nor does it contain toxins because it 'glues' the intestines together. Ground grains are darkened with as much wheat germ as possible and this is what is cooked. It needs to be cooked, because 90% of the people would choke if they ate the grain uncooked. Cooked grains do not lose their value. They can be consumed and will not fatigue the brain.

There are two reasons for eating like this: vitamins taken from nature will not be lost nor will the body have to fight to assimilate them.

I always maintained the theory not to consume chemicals. We particularly succeeded in this because we recognized the value of fasting.

I always ask a sick person when he gets up in the morning to eat grains with milk, and a spoonful of honey. (However, I do not fight against the morning cigarettes and coffee, against those habits, which have come to us from the East.) In this way, he receives the energy to maintain his activity without problems for up to five hours. He is able to remain active (walking, running, rowing, etc.) This particular way of nutrition produces a lot of energy, and it is due only to the portion or amount of the grains. In the evening, I suggest that he only take buttermilk. This is good for the brain, which influences sleep during the night. The brain produces acid, thus creating a mixture that facilitates the lubrication of joints and organs. During the course of the night, while he sleeps, acid is produced also in the stomach which is both a plague and a medicine. However, because of bacteria in the buttermilk, this acid is broken down. The consumption of grains is medicinal while the consumption of coffee and cigarettes also produces acid; acid on acid leads to sickness, which is what can cause cancer. As we all know, cancer is a life-threatening disease.

An eastern doctor asserts that we have neglected fat in the diet. Pig fat (lard) does not produce fats in the body; rather, fats are produced from dried products. It would be good to put a spoonful of lard into foods. Since fat and suet are diminishing from our tables, intestinal and stomach cancers are appearing. Oil, however, is a preservative and a toxin. When foods are cooked, the toxin from the oil is activated even more so. By avoiding such foods and eating breakfast as I said, one guards his health. In the light of our theory, breakfast is the most important meal. Lunch is second and dinner should consist of something light. One can live very simply, by adding milk and honey into their diet.

According to this theory, what can be said about sweets and chocolate?

Today they are not so dangerous. There exists a sweet that is made without preservatives. This sweet is made from grains and from a sea algae which produces jelly and liquefies fruit. The sea algae must be cooked with the grain and it can be poured over fruit. However, when it is dried, it forms a type of cake, which is not baked, but can be eaten as is. There are no types of toxins in this cake. All of the various ingredients added to sweets such as yeast, acid salts and other preservatives, which are no good and toxic, are omitted. The organism remains much healthier if preservatives are not used.

Add a little honey, which is a natural form of sweetness to everything and this ensures that there is no danger. As soon as refined sugar is added, the danger exists of placing a lot of stress on the liver, pancreas and digestion. Refined sugar raises the insulin level, inhibiting the release of certain hormones which in turn weakens the immune system. That is why the natural sweetness of wheat, oats and sugar cane can also be used. This natural sweetness does not have the same effect on the organism as refined sugar. It provides vitamins, minerals and proteins which stabilizes the blood sugar and aides in digestion. Wheat germ is also sweet and sugar is produced from it.

What can be said about meat and meat products, other foods and drug products?

JS: The most dangerous group of foods is beer. It has poisoned all of our people who lived and worked in Germany. Many got rich on beer by poisoning others. Beer is the best preservative because it can never spoil. The bottle can stay open, and it will not get rancid.

Another risk group is carbonated drinks like Coca-Cola and Pepsi. Such drinks contain one toxin - caffeine - which is extracted from tobacco. It takes five liters of extract to make 500 liters of Coca-Cola. That is the most damaging drug, destroying the liver and the urinary tract. Much is lost sexually because of this as well. Many people have cirrhosis of the liver: they never drank alcohol or smoked, but they did drink Coca-Cola.

Healthy replacements of drinks are water, tea (from any herb), and homemade wine. By real home-made wine, I don't mean bottled wine in which yeast can't be produced, because even from our worst wine, it can be produced. Sadly, we have to fight to return to home-made wine and use other home-made nutritional products.

The third risk group are salamis and cheeses which contain preservatives. These cheeses are made from potato and starch. They are not of the same quality as home-made cheese.

In the other risk group belong all foods that are fried. Oil used contains 3% toxins and during frying, the toxins increase to 40%. Everything else that is produced is full of preservatives and so is dangerous for the organism.

As a man involved with nutritional problems, what do you think about Our Lady asking for two days of a life with bread and water?

JS: Our Lady is right. Water is advisable in every diet for losing weight, but if people eat in a way that I mentioned and drink four glasses of water before sleeping, they will stay healthy.

With regards to integral bread, one can live on it an entire week without any problems. What is in the grain is also in the bread and a person can eat it without losing any nutrition. Stored fats and Vitamins A, B, E, and D are present and sufficient for the organism to maintain energy and also for digestion. With this food, nothing is lost. It is important not to overeat after the fast. Rather we need to eat kidney beans, green beans and root vegetables in compensation. In this way, all needs are met. When the digestion system is in order, than one knows that their nutrition is fine and that they are healthy.

We must try to inspire people to accept Our Lady's call for two reasons: fasting would help individuals on a physical level and as a nation, overall, fasting would help it to become more aware and less nervous.

13.2. Fasting and Physical Health

It is a well-known fact that the nutrition of many individuals is dependent on their personal health and vice versa. It is said that a person who eats normally consumes one-third more than he actually needs. This excess presents a large burden on the organism and it is harmed because of this surplus of food. The organism is weakened and gets sick more easily.

This is why it is good to fast even if a person does not believe or seek a spiritual dimension. Therapeutic fasting is offered more frequently in order for the organism to be unburdened and for the physical health to be restored. (see text pertaining to Dr. Mayr's fasting therapy.)

When a person returns to health at least partially and decides to fast it is very important that he alter his manner of nutrition. If he doesn't change his way of eating, he will find himself in a vicious circle. He will gain weight and get sick and then have to go through weeks of therapeutic fasting for weight loss, liberation and healing of the organism. The victims of this vicious circle are especially those individuals who undertake various diet therapies for weight loss.

It would be best for a person who has decided to undergo a therapeutic fast for any physical reason to, at the same time, learn and accept a new way of nutrition. Consequently, on the following pages, I have included elementary information about healthy food, about essentials for the organism, and how such needs can best be met.

13.3. What is Necessary for the Human Organism

FOOD, WATER, AIR, AND SUNLIGHT represent the essentials for human survival. Their mutual functions give energy, which is carried out in every part of our bodies. Food is not only an element of nourishment, which our bodies need to be satisfied: it is necessary for development, maintenance and duration of life. It is necessary for health, for resistance, for working ability, for our looks, for our disposition, and for our happiness. An increased knowledge about nutrition will facilitate in planning more varied meals, which will include all healthy and nutritional components. Many of the numerous particulars you come across serve only as an orientation about calories and of the value of individual components. These specifics vary from source to source. This is not unusual considering the impact on the value of a particular component (i.e. the soil in which it was grown, the climate, the conditions from planting to cultivation, the time of harvest, processing, care, and preparation.)

The three basic compounds from which our bodies draw energy (calories) are proteins, carbohydrates, and fats. One portion of the calories is essential for the processes within the organism itself, for its maintenance and life. The other portion is necessary for psychological and physical activity. These three compounds, together with water, are essential for the organism in larger quantities, while vitamins, minerals, and rock elements are needed in far lesser quantities.

THE DAILY NEED OF CALORIES ranges on the average from 2,500 to 3,000 calories. Those participating in strenuous physical activities and athletes who are engaged in intense training need up to 4,000 to 5,000 calories. Because we are not all built the same, we are not equally active and the conditions of our organisms vary (age and development, pregnancy, old age, disease). Therefore, we require different quantities of calories. However, the calories in their composition, without considering the quantities, must contain all of the elements necessary for the human body.

The composition of these calories must be represented by the basic food components. The reciprocal reactions and the unfolding of the process of the metabolism depend on the proportion and relationship of these constituent components in the overall daily calorie intake.

Proteins:	80-100 g	(1g=4.1 calories)
Carbohydrates:	100-360 g	(1g=4.1 calories)
Fats:	60-100 g	(1g=9.3 calories)

These constituent elements contain:

- **vitamins, minerals, and rock elements**

- **oxygen** is the most important part of air and is indispensable in all levels of metabolism. Respiration is indispensable for all life functions.

- **water** is an integral part of the human body, and like food and other liquids, it has a significant role in dissolving nutritional components and transmitting them from the digestive organs through the bloodstream to each cell. Water serves to eliminate unessential and harmful substances from the body.

Metabolism is a term for all chemical processes, which take place in our organisms, from the eating and the breaking down of food to the elimination of waste material from the body. Our body is not able to use the valuable components of food in the quantities in which we ingest them. Rather, with the help of enzymes it breaks them down into the smallest components so that through the mucus membrane of the intestines, it may proceed to the blood and the lymphatic system to supply nutrition to every cell of the organism.

The disruption of the metabolism can take place in several ways:

- because of an excessive enjoyment of foods rich in calories: that is, by mainly eating depleted, refined foods which do not contain sufficient vitamins, minerals, enzymes, and other valuable elements

- because of a poor choice of ingredients in meals and irregular and improper meal times which impede the course of digestion

- because of different illnesses which can be the cause, but can also be a consequence of a disruption of the metabolism

Enzymes are digestive juices produced by glands in the mouth (saliva), in the stomach, in the pancreas, and in the thin mucus of the small intestine. In this way the juices take part in very harmonious chemical processes and each of them has their own role in digestion. Vitamins induce their secretion. It is important to realize that digestion begins in the mouth. Thoroughly chewed food that is saturated with saliva, the digestive juices in the mouth, is more easily digested. This is especially applicable to starch, because its breakdown already begins in the mouth.

Hormones are chemical regulators which, together with the nervous system, prompt or block physical functions and affect all metabolic processes. Hormones are produced by glands with internal secretion: thyroid gland, parathyroid glands, the pancreas, the pituitary gland, thymus gland, and sexual glands.

Proteins represent the building materials of each living organism and so also, of our bodies. During the course of digestion, proteins from food breakdown to amino acids from which the organism creates its own essential proteins. The body cannot produce some of the essential amino acids on its own. It is required for them to be brought in by way of food. The increase of quantities of proteins will not improve their composition, but the great waste in the metabolism will unnecessarily burden the organism.

DAILY ESSENTIAL PROTEIN: 80-100g (26.8 - 33.5 ounces.)

It is considered that 0.8-1g (.03-.33 ounces) of protein is sufficient for each 2.2 pounds of human weight. Up to 120g (40 ounces) is sufficient for those undergoing greater physical exertion, and for pregnant and nursing mothers.

Sources: plant and animal origin, especially soy and its products, sunflower seeds, sesame seeds, green beans, walnuts, cereals, fresh cheese. Plant sources of protein 100g (33.5 ounces): granular soy and soy flour 37g (12.4 ounce), soy cheese 5g (1.7 ounces), other beans ranging from 20- 23g (6.7-7.7 ounces), pumpkin seeds 32g (10.7 ounces), linseed 24g (8.0 ounces), sunflowers 27g (9.0 ounces), sesame 20g (6.7 ounces), almond 18g (6.0 ounces), walnuts and hazelnuts 14g (4.7 ounces), peanuts 26g (8.7 ounces), cereals 10-15g (3.4-5.0 ounces.)

In order to fulfill the needs of the organism, proteins in food would need to be represented by **1/3 from animal sources** (eggs, milk products, meat and fish) and **2/3 from plant sources** (beans: soy, dried lentil, chick peas, kidney beans), walnuts, almonds, hazelnuts, green vegetables and fruit.

All essential amino acids are contained in animal proteins, in that way, they are considered 'complete.' Because of this, they have been given great significance, which has resulted in many dietary mistakes. Only 150g (50.25 ounces) of meat can satisfy the daily protein need and this is significant from an economic prospective. Meat is the most expensive source of protein. Nutritionally, soy is a proper meat substitute and is much cheaper. Moreover, a quart of milk contains more valuable nutrients than a piece of meat purchased for the same amount of money.

Even if you are not a vegetarian, there is no reason why you must eat meat at every meal every day. When you prepare a meal with a good combination of plant proteins, meat is not necessary. However, if you insist, along with that, you need no more than 25-30g (8.4-10.0 ounces) of animal proteins contained in 100-150g (33.5-50.25 ounces) of edible meat portions. If you eat meat, you should always give preference to fish and poultry. It is sufficient to eat meat one or two times a week. Generally, preference should be given to plant proteins because they also contain other valuable elements that meat does not. They are also not prone to quick deterioration like animal proteins. Plant proteins are easier to digest, and in breaking down do not create large quantities of toxins in the organism. They do not contain damaging cholesterol.

Components of amino acids in plant ingredients are not equal and plant proteins are considered 'incomplete.' Therefore, it is necessary to consider food combinations in order to secure all essential amino acids for the body. If there is insufficient protein intake, the body will draw necessary proteins from ones' own body tissue, resulting in diminished muscle mass and energy loss.

Important amino acids are found in apples, strawberries, figs, oranges, peaches, grapes, cow's milk, mother's milk, green beans, potatoes, soy, peanuts, whole grain oats, barley, corn, and whole grain flour with bran from other cereals.

CARBOHYDRATES, like fats, give the body energy and warmth. A carbohydrate is a combination of sugar and starch that an organism converts into sugar. However, there is a big difference in the ways in which our body makes use of them.

1. SUGAR - refined white – is a source of empty calories because it does not contain a single substance necessary for the organism. It enters the bloodstream directly and quickly in quantities greater than the body can use at that moment. It has been noted that it has a negative influence on assimilation of minerals and vitamins. Sugar and foods with a high sugar content (cakes, sweets, candies, overly sweetened juices and drinks) use a greater quantity of proteins, vitamins and minerals for their own breakdown (especially vitamin B), and they stress the liver. Sugar makes it impossible to utilize calcium and magnesium, which causes the softening of bones and the rotting of teeth. Because of this, care should be taken regarding nutritional balance for children. If the use of sugar is unavoidable, refined sugars and foods that contain refined sugar should be avoided. When using sugar, it is preferable to use brown cane sugar. Marmalade is also preferred in relation to refined sugars because, in addition to sugar, it contains other valuable ingredients.

Natural sugar has a positive effect on our health, because, in addition to sugar and starch, it contains many other nutritional elements and fiber. Only fruit sugar – fructose - can be considered a dietetic food. Because the body utilizes it more slowly, sudden increases in blood sugar are avoided. **The best sources of fructose are fruits, vegetables, and natural honey.** Sugars from honey contain predominantly 75% fructose and introduce a natural concentrate with more than 100 biologically valuable elements, especially calcium and iron.

Grape sugar - glucose is found in fruit (grapes contain 20-30%.) However, the grape sugar which can be obtained in tablet or powder form does not come from grapes, but from potato and cornstarch.

2. STARCH is the main ingredient found in grains and beans. By means of enzymes, it is converted into sugar, but by a slower process. Its entry into the blood stream is gradual. In that way the body's energy and warmth are secured over a longer period of time during the course of a day with regular continuity.

DAILY ESSENTIAL CARBOHYDRATES: 100-360g (33.5-121 ounces)

Sources: dried beans and cereals, fruit, vegetables, honey, sugar, sweetened juices and drinks, and also various sweets and cakes.

– 100g (33.5 ounces) of grain contains around 300-500 kcal

– 100g (33.5 ounces) of honey: 315 kcal

– 100g (33.5 ounces) of sugar: 390 kcal, 1 tsp. full contains 30 kcal.

Carbohydrates are a fuel and an exceptional source of energy that increases the ability to work. However, it is preferable to derive the necessary carbohydrates from dried beans and grains, as well as vegetables and fruits. These sources represent a good source of vitamins, minerals, and plant fibers. Food that is very rich in carbohydrates and poor in protein hinders the formation of important enzymes for digestion that are created in the pancreas.

Those who avoid starchy foods because of calories are mistaken. If a diet does not contain sufficient carbohydrates, the body uses its own proteins and fats, causing tissue and organ deterioration, starting with the muscles. Although it is not necessary to omit sugar entirely from a diet, only the amount that body can use should be consumed. Fatty acids result from excess sugar and they accumulate in the organism in the form of fat. It is not only sugar and starch that cause weight gain. Excess calories from general food intake can do the same.

It is especially important for this group of foods that secure essential carbohydrates for the body, to be unrefined. When they are unrefined, they retain more vitamins, minerals and plant fibers. It is best to substitute regular sweets with fresh or dried fruits and with whole grain fruitcakes and cookies. It is possible to sweeten with ground raisins instead of sugar.

FATS are irreplaceable substances our organisms need for creating energy and warmth. They are indispensable for breaking down fat soluble Vitamins A, D, E, K. At the same time they improve the composition and taste of food creating a feeling of fullness.

DAILY ESSENTIAL FATS: 60-100g (20.1-33.5 ounces)

Those undergoing strenuous physical activity and exposed to cold need a greater fat intake. It is recommended that the sick and elderly reduce their intake of fatty foods especially animal fats. Excess of fat in a diet causes poor use of sugar. However, being overweight is not exclusively a consequence of fat in the diet. The body also creates fat from the excess intake of other foods because of overeating.

Sources: plant and animal fats.

Contents of fat in 100g (33.5 ounces) of food:

- margarine, butter, mayonnaise, lard, plant fat, vegetable oil: about 80-100%. Various fatty cheeses: about 45-60%. Olives: 95%; almonds: 81%; peanuts: 75%; soy: 40%.

- other plant foods generally contain a low level of fat

The body is unable to produce some unsaturated fats and so they must be provided through food. For this reason, best quality fats should be used.

In order of quality, fats can be categorized into three groups:

1. **Cold filtered oils:** olive, sunflower, soy, almonds, walnuts, hazelnuts, peanuts, fish oils and hydrogenated plant fats retain all useful substances, smells, and tastes in their natural form

2. **Milk fats:** butter, cream, and other full fat dairy products

3. **Solid fats** (especially lard) and warm filtered oil, fatty meats (brain, liver, and chest glands), egg yolks. These fats contain greater quantities of saturated fat and cholesterol and should be avoided or used sparingly

It is not easy to establish an ideal quantity of fat a person needs in his diet. Some think that grains, fruits, and vegetables contain sufficient amounts of fat needed and that fat should not be added to food. Instead, foods containing fat and oil should be chosen. Plant oils, regardless of how healthy they are, should be used in moderation.

It is important to consider that fat contains 9.3 kcal, while proteins and carbohydrates contain half as much - 4.1 kcal. Fat is found in various pastries, cakes rich in butter and egg yolks, in fatty cheeses, whole fat milk products, seeds and various dressings. Fruits and vegetables also contain a certain amount of fat.

WATER comprises about 70-75% of the human body and is an indispensable and an integral component of all tissue. From that, its significance to our organism is evident. It dissolves and absorbs nutritional elements from food, and it transports them through the blood stream then from the digestive system to every cell. After the exchange, the unnecessary and harmful substances are eliminated from the body. Because of that, the organism continually needs water. It is essential to drink a proper amount of it each day.

NECESSARY DAILY WATER INTAKE: 2-3 quarts

Water is ingested through food products (approximately 1 quart). The rest must be taken in by fluids. For adults, that would be about 6-8 glasses. This is a minimum essential amount required for proper kidney functioning and for the removal of toxins and waste products from the body. Those engaged in hard physical labor and subject to intense heat, may need up to 10 liters (with an addition of salt if there is great perspiration.)

Sources: The best is pure water, spring water if possible, but natural fruit and vegetable juices and milk are also recommended. Natural minerals need to be added to purified and distilled water, if it is intended for drinking, (2 to 3 teaspoons of sea salt per quart of water.) Non-carbonated and Oligocene mineral water can be useful for various malfunctions of the metabolism and of digestion. They regulate stomach functions and help with gall bladder disorders and cleanse the organism.

Water should become a natural drink and a daily habit, especially for small children. A child's developing organism is susceptible to disorder that is balanced out by water. This is often the cause of various illnesses where the child is not aware of his need for liquids. Therefore, it is necessary to offer and encourage the children to drink during the course of the day without forcing them. In kindergarten, more attention should be dedicated to creating such a habit. Unfortunately, it is often there that this element important for life is denied because to satisfy this need would create extra work. Natural water is a food, a remedy and a source of many minerals. It has no undesirable side effects regardless of the high content of lime and minerals. Minerals from natural water are well utilized by the body. They do not cause kidney stones, hardened and blocked arteries or other similar illnesses.

Coffee, real tea (Russian or Chinese), and different cola drinks cannot substitute for water, because they contain caffeine which speeds up the elimination of liquids from the body.

OXYGEN is an element without which, there would not be life on earth. It is the most important component of air and is necessary at all levels of metabolism. The basic condition of life is breathing – a continuous supply of oxygen to the organism. With increased physical activity, we intake more oxygen into our blood stream through the lungs and we exhale carbon dioxide. This is the external form of breathing while the same process takes place within the cells of the organism. The cause of damaging the functions of certain organs and of the entire organism is often directly related to the insufficiencies of the air we breathe. Moreover, increased concentrations of carbon dioxide are the cause of many sicknesses and even death. Often we are not aware that this is actually the cause of our headaches, fatigue or weakness. **AIR, SUN, AND LIGHT** are the sources of life. That is why more time needs to be spent in nature and there needs to be more exercise and physical activity. This will positively affect all of the processes in our organism and all of the valuable components of our nutrition will be put to best use.

VITAMINS are highly active organic substances contained in valuable proteins, fats and carbohydrates of various foods. Every vitamin has a different function and together they influence numerous chemical processes in our body. Their deficiency brings about various disorders that can be noticed on the skin, hair, nails and throughout the systems of the body.

When a vitamin deficiency is determined, it is rare that only one vitamin is lacking. On the basis of recent research, it is determined that Vitamins C, B1, A, and E are most frequently lacking. With malignancies, Vitamins A, C, and E are most often missing.

Ingredients of Bread

Bread is a necessary food and an integral part of daily nutrition. Therefore, it needs to be given definite importance. In deciding whether to eat dark bread or whole grain wheat or other grains, one must look for the sources which maintain the quality of nutrition and health. The darker the bread, the healthier it is.

Dark bread contains three to ten times more minerals and vitamins and two to three times more calcium and Vitamin B1 than white bread. Proteins in dark bread are of greater value than in white or semi-white breads because they contain wheat germ and bran. Daily essentials of Vitamin B can be satisfied with 250g (83.75 ounces) of dark bread. To receive the same amount of Vitamin B from white bread, 1.5 kg of it would need to be consumed. White bread is filling, but does not have the same proteins, minerals, or vitamins as darker breads.

- 50g (16.75 ounces) of white bread has 130 kcal; 50g (16.75 ounces) of dark bread has 108 kcal; 50g (16.75 ounces) of toast has 100 kcal; 50g (16.75 ounces) of rye has 120 kcal; 50 g (16.75 ounces) of soy has 101 kcal.

Preparing bread

Preparation is very simple. Making bread is perceived as a big task, but there are some elementary procedures and ingredients.

Flour – For bread, medium ground wheat flour is best. Continual usage of bread from 100% wheat flour is not the best, because it can be enriched by an addition of other grains, seeds and wheat germ. Wheat flour in greater quantity should always be given priority.

Yeast – Whether fresh or dry, yeast is used to leaven the bread and to facilitate digestion. Moisture and warmth activate fungal yeast, expanding the dough up to four times in volume. Because of this, bread needs to be baked well to avoid undesirable expansion in the intestines. A temperature greater than 49ºC (120ºF) stops fungal activity. Yeast combined with a spoonful of sugar and some flour should always be mixed separately to start the fermentation process. A small amount of sugar added to yeast speeds up fermentation while a large amount slows it down. Yeast is the healthiest means of leavening dough. Baking soda and baking powder are not, because they destroy the Vitamin B complex and stimulate the bile ducts.

Substitutes for yeast – If yeast is not available, a left over piece of unbaked dough can be added for leavening. Alternatively 150g (50.25 ounces) of sugar, 50g (16.75 ounces) of white flour and a teaspoonful of salt can be mixed in ½ liter (1.05 pints) of water. Cook for one hour at low temperature, stirring occasionally. Use for leavening bread only after 12 hours or the next day.

Water and warmth – the temperature of water plays an important role because it can be neither too cold nor too hot. It is best at 45ºC (113ºF.)

Salt – improves the taste of bread, but can be left out for health reasons in preparation of unsalted bread. It is best for salt to be dissolved in some lukewarm water and for salted water to be added to flour (salt slows down yeast activity.) To each kilogram (2.2 pounds) of plain flour, 1.5 dkg of salt and 1 dkg of yeast can be added. When using white flour, more salt (2 dkg) and yeast (2 dkg) should be added.

Oil – is not indispensable, but when added makes bread soft and prevents it from drying out. Add a small amount, perhaps a tablespoon. The dough is kneaded for ten minutes and must become 'satiny' and smooth.

Different Supplements to Wheat Flour Bread

- **corn flour –** is mixed with water and brought to a boil, then cooled and added to the remaining flour

- **coarse oat flour** – is added to boiling water, cooled not to damage the yeast and then added to flour

- **oat flakes** – are covered with boiling water, set aside for 20 minutes to expand; and then added to flour

- **soy flour** – 95% of wheat is mixed with 5% of soy flour. Although soy is an excellent addition which increases protein value, greater quantities make bread heavy

- **other supplements** – cooked grain wheat or dried fruits and raisins are added to the dough after all other ingredients have been mixed and the dough is ready for raising

After the dough is mixed, it is sprinkled with flour, covered with a cloth and left to rise at temperatures ranging from 23 -27º Celsius (73 – 81ºF). After one or two hours, when the dough has risen sufficiently, all the air bubbles are taken out and the dough is shaped into a desired form without being rolled out. It is left to rise again in greased bread pans for a short while because it will continue to rise in the oven. Before being placed in the oven, the dough is glazed with some water, so that the crust will be more pliable. Bake the bread in the oven approximately 45 minutes at 180º Celsius (355ºF). It is done when it is light or when it makes a hollow sound when tapped with a finger.

Problems that Can Arise

1. *Sour taste* – causes: water is too hot, the temperature while rising is too high, poor quality of yeast or to long a time left for rising

2. *Dry bread* – causes: baked for too long or too much flour was added

3. *'Doughy' bread* – causes: too much liquid or insufficient baking time

Different Kinds Of Bread

- **Homemade bread** – to lukewarm water add 1.5 kg (3.30 pounds) of sifted flour, 30 g (10.05 ounces) of yeast and salt (1 teaspoon.) Knead the dough on a floured board until it is firm and elastic. After rising, it should be baked for 45 minutes.

- **Mixed rye bread** – smooth dough is made from 600g (201 ounces) of rye and 400g (124 ounces) of wheat flour, mixed with 1 packet of dried yeast, a little salt and 6 dl of lukewarm water. The dough is covered with a cloth and let rise for 30 minutes. After rising, it should be baked for 70 minutes at 200° Celsius (390°F).

- **Bran Bread** – smooth dough is made from 500g (167.5 ounces) of bran and 1 packet of dried yeast to which the following mixture is added: 75g (25.13 ounces) of bran, 75g (25.13 ounces) of oat flakes and 75g (25.13 ounces) of ground flax seeds, 1 egg, 50g (16.75 ounces) of softened butter or margarine, 3.5 dl of lukewarm milk and a little salt. Mixed dough is left to rise in a warm temperature. Bake for 45 minutes at 180° Celsius (355°F).

- **Herbal Bread** – smooth dough is made from 500g (167.5 ounces) of flour, 1 packet of yeast, 125g (41.88 ounces) of oat flakes, 50g (16.75 ounces) of softened butter or margarine, 1 egg, 3 dl of lukewarm milk and salt. Work into the dough an additional 2 tablespoons of fine minced herbs and sprouts (parsley, celery, onion, brewers yeast, wheat germ and alfalfa.) The dough is left to stand for 30 minutes until it rises. Before baking, the top is sprinkled with oat flakes. The bread is baked for 40 minutes at 180º Celsius (355ºF).

- **Corn Bread** – Firm dough is made from 250g (83.75 ounces) of corn flour (prepared as directed), 1 kg (2.2 pounds) of white flour, yeast, oil and salt. The bread is shaped and put into a warm place to rise. It is baked for about 1 hour at 150º Celsius (300º F).

- **Unleavened Bread** – 2 cups of whole wheat flour, 1 cup of buckwheat flour, 1.5 spoonful's of sea salt are mixed into a dough. The dough is divided into thirds and baked in greased pans at 150º Celsius (300º F).

Baking Powder Bread, Flat Bread and Fried Bread

- **Baking Powder Bread** – 18 tablespoons of flour, ½ teaspoon of salt, 1 package of baking powder, 1 cup of yogurt, 1 tablespoon oil and 2 eggs. Eggs and salt are blended with a mixer, oil and yogurt are added and mixed again. Dry ingredients are added and the dough is baked in greased pans, in a pre-heated oven at 200º Celsius (390ºF). After baking, the bread can be brushed with oil, wrapped in foil and cooled.

- **Baking Powder Bread With Mineral Water** – 1 kg (2.2 pounds) of flour, 2 eggs, 1 tablespoon of baking powder and 1 liter (1.06 quarts) of mineral water are mixed together until a smooth dough is formed. It is baked until golden.

- **Simple Flat Bread With Cheese** - Beat 3 eggs, add one cup of buttermilk, 1 cup of oil, 1 teaspoon of salt, 18 tablespoons of flour and 200g (67 ounces) of cottage cheese and mix well. Pans are greased and the bread is baked for about a half an hour.

- **Fast Baking Powder Bread** – Mix 500g (167.5 ounces) of flour, 1 tablespoon of baking powder, 1 teaspoon of salt with 1 cup of yogurt. Shape the dough into 4 cakes and bake on a greased pan for about 15 minutes at 250º Celsius (480ºF).

- **Fried Yeast Bread** – Mix 500g (167.5 ounces) of flour with 10g (3.35 ounces) of leavened yeast, 1-2 eggs, a little water and salt. Let the dough stand in a warm place (in a double boiler over warm water.) Roll out and fry strips of dough in hot oil.

- **Baking Powder Fried Bread** – Combine 2 eggs, a cup of buttermilk, ½ tablespoon of baking powder, a little salt, a cup of oil and enough flour to make a soft dough. The dough is scooped by the spoonful and grilled in hot oil.

- **Sweet Baking Powder Bread** – Can be quickly prepared by mixing 1 cup of yogurt, 2 cups of flour, ½ tablespoon of baking powder, 1 egg, 1 tablespoon of sugar and a some salt. Drop spoonful's of dough into hot oil to fry. When cool, sprinkle with sugar.

- **Peasant Fried Bread** – Sift and salt 100-150g (33.5-50.25 ounces) of wheat flour, add 3-4 whole eggs, 4-5 tablespoons of sugar and add sufficient lukewarm water to achieve the consistency of crape dough. Into hot butter in a frying pan, spoonful's of dough are dropped. They should spread flat and fried until golden brown. When finished, they can be sprinkled with sugar and served hot.

Simple Dough For Different Purposes

Often from the same dough, different meals can be prepared, both sweet and savory, depending on ingredients added or different shapes.

Filo Pastry Dough:

- Mix 250g (83.75 ounces) of margarine, 2 cups of yogurt, 2 tablespoonful's of sugar, some salt and enough flour to be absorbed by the mixture around 500-600g (167.5-201 ounces). Mix until the dough is smooth and form into five balls. Wrap in foil. It can remain for several days in the refrigerator, or longer in the freezer.

- For finer filo pastry, follow this recipe: 500 g (167.5 ounces) of flour mixed with 2 tablespoons of oil and 2.5 dl of salted lukewarm water. Divide the dough into two and knead each part well until smooth and round. Glaze each ball of dough with a little oil and let stand in a warm place for one hour. The dough is then carefully stretched by hand until paper thin on a large flour board. Readymade filo pastry is available for purchase.

Different sweet and salty fillings can be used with this type of dough including various fruits, cheese, sautéed vegetables, ham and meats.

GRAINS contain 65-75% carbohydrates, 10-15% proteins, approximately 4% fat (found only in wheat germ) and vitamins and minerals (mainly in the exterior cover of wheat.) Therefore, only whole wheat and whole wheat products, rich in Vitamin B complex, Vitamin E, calcium, magnesium, iron and fiber, have a significant meaning in human nutrition.

Bread and other grain products are a basic food for nearly all of mankind. If they are from whole grains they contain nearly all that an organism needs, except for Vitamin C. They are suitable for all meal combinations with milk and milk products, seeds, different fresh and dried fruits and vegetables. This makes a variety of meals possible. Diets rich in grain and bread from whole wheat regulate the levels of cholesterol in the blood, while also shielding against arteriosclerosis and heart attacks. They act as a successful remedy and prevention against a variety of illnesses. Nutrition depends on the manner of preparation and the quality of the grains used.

All grains are similar in their make-up. Their components can be divided into three main parts:

1. **Bran** (outside cover) contains fiber and a number of minerals and vitamins

2. **Starch** (the middle part of the grain) contains mainly starch with some protein and traces of minerals and fiber

3. **Wheat germ** (the smallest part of the core) is rich in high quality proteins and fats, not to mention vitamins and minerals whose nutritional value increases with germination

Only natural uniformity between these three parts of the grain give the potency and the nutritional value expected from grains. The products or flour containing all these components are called integral. In industrial treatment and grinding, bran and wheat germ are eliminated and in that way, so are numerous nutritional components. All that remains is starch with some proteins.

In this process, grains actually lose those vitamins and minerals, which are essential for their exchange of substance and for the digestion process. The reason that bran and wheat germ are eliminated in processing is because of spoiling. Whole grain can retain its components for a long period of time. Crushing reduces that period while grinding quickens the loss of value. The value of freshly ground raw grains, especially of wheat and rye, is exceptional.

Each grain has its own distinctions and differences in composition of amino acids. That it why it is good to combine several grains. If only one grain is used, a meal should also include milk products or legumes.

Dr. Kollarth recommends that before every other meal 40-50g (13.4 -16.75 ounces) of grains be taken daily with dried fruit, walnuts and hazelnuts and freshly grated apple, softened with a little water, cream, milk or yogurt.

In the summer, a cold tea can be prepared from grains (barley, rice, and whole wheat) that are roasted in a pan for 10 minutes as they are stirred continually. To 1.5 liters (1.59 quarts) of cold water, two or three spoonful's of roasted ground grain is added and brought to a boil for 10 minutes at high temperature. This tea is drunk filtered and cooled. It works to cleanse toxins from the body and it is considered of special medicinal value.

WHEAT – *TRITICUM VULGARE* - **100g (33.5 ounces) = 342 kcal**. Rich in minerals and vitamins. It is high in phosphorous, and contains potassium, calcium, magnesium, iron and other essential elements. It is the only grain with Provitamin A. It contains the entire Vitamin B complex, in addition to Vitamins E, D, and K that are found only in whole grains. Various types of wheat differ in their content of amino acids, vitamins and minerals. Sadly, in order to increase the shelf life of wheat flour essential oils are removed because they spoil easily. In that way, valuable vitamin and mineral components are also lost. Integral wheat is one of the most valuable grains, not just as a food, but also for its medicinal value. Pulp of fresh ground wheat is recommended (after soaking for a few hours in water) for bettering digestion, increasing work ability and decreasing fatigue. It is also recommended as an aid for regular digestion, a combatant against heart disease, for cleansing skin and prevents premature aging.

Grain wheat derived from pulp is used to cleanse the body of toxic substances. It also used against various stomach and intestinal ailments, and it is recommended to stop diarrhea. The simplest way to use whole wheat grain is to cook in a closed pot after it has soaked until every grain has burst. While cooking, only enough boiling water is added to maintain steam and prevent scorching. Some salt is added only at the end of cooking. Cooked wheat can be added to:

- spinach, Swiss chard or another green vegetable with olive oil

- legumes and other grains (cooked wheat, chick peas, barley with olive oil)

- stewed, dried or fresh fruit

- milk or dairy products – with some honey

- ground walnuts, almonds, hazelnuts, etc.

RYE - *SECALE CEREALE* - **100g (33.5 ounces)** = **349 kcal**. It is rich in minerals. It is high in potassium, phosphorous and magnesium and contains more iron and calcium than wheat. It is high in Vitamin B, and is rich in carbohydrates, proteins and fiber while containing low fat. Along with wheat, it is the only grain that does not need to be crushed but is eaten baked and uncrushed. Rye flour is useful in improving the nutritional value of bread made from other grains, for making sauces, for thickening soups, and for vegetable dishes. All parts of the rye grain contain medicinal value. Rye bread is recommended daily both for those who are healthy and those who suffer with arteriosclerosis, poor blood circulation, high blood pressure, migraine headaches, menopause and nerve problems. Those with anemia can also include rye sprouts in their diet. Pure rye bread is not soft and porous like wheat bread, therefore, a mixture of grain flours is recommended.

OATS - *AVENA SATIVA* - **100g (33.5 ounces) = 308 kcal.** Contain all 18 amino acids (like animal proteins) and carbohydrates without much fat. They contain enough lecithin and all of the most important vitamins; Provitamin A, B1, B2, B6, E, K, and biotin. Oats are rich in minerals, especially calcium, phosphorous, magnesium, iron, copper, manganese, zinc, sodium, sulfur, fluoride, boron, and iodine. Many memory problems in children are attributed to a deficiency of phosphorous. Tests show that phosphorous has a positive influence on the functioning of brain cells, lecithin for nerve activity and iron for fortifying blood. Oats are rich in proteins used for rebuilding and growth of the organism. Because of their composition, Kneipp and many others have recommended oats in the daily diets of children in their development and have especially recommended oat flakes for breakfast. As a most medicinal grain, oats are recommended to fight against general exhaustion of the organism, depression, tuberculosis, against inflammation in the joints, and for kidney, liver and stomach. Oats can be used as whole grain, rolled, crushed, flaked, semolina or flour. Since oat sprouts go bad quickly and become bitter, they need to be eaten fresh. The flour is useful for preparing bread, buns, and as an addition to a variety of other dishes.

Oat flakes and groats (husked ground oats) can be used uncooked: a spoonful of oats is soaked in two tablespoons of water for 15 minutes with some honey or lemon juice added. A small quantity of this can be taken during the course of the day. Oat flakes should not be cooked for more than five minutes, because they start to lose their valuable ingredients. The water in which oats are cooked should not be thrown out because it contains medicinal substances. Milk or cream can be added. Oats cooked in the consistency of soup or porridge are especially recommended after stomach and intestinal surgery.

BARLEY - *HORDEUM VULGARE* - **100g (33.5 ounces) = 317 kcal**. The biological value of barley is nearly the same as that of whole wheat. It is rich in phosphorous, calcium, magnesium, sulfur, iron, manganese, cobalt, copper, zinc, fluoride, iodine, and essential fatty acids. Of all the grains, barley contains the most Vitamin E, nearly all of the Vitamin B complex, and Vitamins A and D. Because of its mineral components, it is recommended as an additive to a tea which enriches the organism with minerals and contributes to its strength and rejuvenation.

Husking barley grains diminishes the value of proteins and fats, while increasing carbohydrates. This form of husked barley is normally used. It needs to be used more often in various combinations with vegetables and seasonings. Barley flour is useful for making white sauces and for making bread in combination with other grains. Since it is high in gluten, barley bread does not rise. However, combined with wheat and yeast it makes a light and tasty bread. By means of processing barley, malt beer is produced. By roasting barley, a coffee substitute is produced such as 'Kneipp coffee'. It is especially recommended for children. Strained barley porridge from cooked barley, diluted with a broth of fresh vegetables and some butter, is recommended in a daily diet for children, together with 'Kneipp coffee' and milk. A thick barley porridge with milk helps increase the production of mother's milk, lessens cholesterol in the blood, and diminishes the illnesses of the gallbladder, liver, and heart. It also helps with problems concerning circulation, rheumatism, diabetes and premature aging. Barley, like whole wheat, can be combined with fresh and dried fruit, stews, hazelnuts and almonds, milk, cream and vegetables.

RICE - *ORYZA SATIVA* - **100g (33.5 ounces)** = **386 kcal**. Its largest content is starch (70-80%). It contains a high quality of proteins, but in smaller quantities than all other grains. It is rich in minerals and high in phosphorus, potassium, magnesium, calcium, manganese, iron, sulfur, zinc, cobalt and fluoride. Its highest content of Vitamin E is found in the germ root, while the Vitamin B complex is found in the covering. That is why glazing and husking reduces its value although it makes it easily digestible. White rice aids in the functioning of the intestines if it is properly prepared without excess starch. It is recommended for the digestive organ ailments, especially for diarrhea. In treatment of high blood pressure boiled unsalted rice, two to three times a day is recommended together with herb tea (mistletoe, hawthorn, and chamomile.) To receive a balanced meal, rice should be served with vegetables and fruit. It is preferable to use unhusked and unglazed (integral) rice, which is more nutritious and contains more cellulose, thus facilitating better elimination in the intestines. Rice can be used as a main meal, as risotto, with a meat and vegetable sauté, in sweet puddings cooked in milk with fresh and dried fruits added, and with different sauces and garnishes.

CORN - *ZEA MAYS* - **100g (33.5 ounces)** = **243 kcal**. Corn is a good source of Vitamins E and B along with many minerals, especially selenium. It contains 80% of carbohydrates (starches and dextrose), and is a source of protein, essential fatty acids and fiber. Corn gives strength and energy to the body. Corn flour is of less biological value than wheat flour. It has Vitamin E and Provitamin A (yellow corn), but does not contain sufficient Vitamin B complex.

Sweet corn is delicious roasted or boiled. Corn flour and corn meal can be used to prepare a variety of sweet and savory side dishes, served with vegetables, especially sauerkraut and tomato based sauces. It can be served with different sauces, nuts or soy, seasoned butter, mayonnaise or sour cream. Because corn flour lacks some essential amino acids, it is good to combine it with other grains, milk or dairy products in order to satisfy nutritional needs. Corn flakes, such as Kellogg's, are an American product, which has retained all essential components of corn. They can be eaten with milk.

Corn silk tea is renowned for its medicinal value regarding all illnesses related to water retention in the tissues. It has been found that corn germ oil is beneficial for the heart muscle and in the treatment of arteriosclerosis, high blood pressure, gout, rheumatism, and the removal of kidney stones.

HUSKED MILLET - *PANICUM MILIACEUM* - **100g (33.5 ounces)** = **327 kcal**. It has a more complete and better balance of proteins than any other grain. It is rich in minerals, especially in iron, magnesium and phosphorous; and also contains Vitamin A and Vitamin B complex (especially B1.) It also contains lecithin, which is indispensable for brain cells, and choline, which protects against arteriosclerosis. It is also important in the maintenance of the nervous system. Millet, as an alkaline grain, is significant in maintaining the intestinal flora (especially after taking antibiotics), and in preventing deterioration of the intestines. Water in which millet is soaked should be used in cooking. It is easily digestible, which is important for children and the elderly. It does not add weight and can be prepared like rice or as a rice substitute. Ground millet mixed with other flours is used in preparation of various pastas, breads, pancakes, and deserts. When it is cooked with milk, raisins, bananas or some other fruits, it provides for a tasty breakfast. It can be prepared with milk as a puree and as a side dish with vegetables. Such a meal should be eaten at least once a week.

A meal with millet and vegetables is recommended twice a week to aid circulatory and intestinal ailments. Millet is an ideal food for both the healthy and the sick, especially for those who have problems with the pancreas and the spleen.

BUCKWHEAT – *FAGOPYRUM ESCULENTUM* - **100g (33.5 ounces)** = **335 kcal**. It has great biological value, because it is very rich in vitamins and minerals. It contains potassium, phosphorous, calcium, magnesium, sodium, iron, and the entire Vitamin B complex. Because it contains Vitamin P (Rutin), it has an effect on the health of the nerve cells, the elasticity of circulatory arteries and capillary resistance. It prevents arteriosclerosis, liver disease, stomach ailments, digestive disorders and high blood pressure.

Buckwheat is not a grain, but because of its chemical components, it is used like grain. It has a strong scent and should be mixed with one or more other grains such as, wheat, rice, corn or millet. Porridge from millet and buckwheat is tasty and nutritional. For porridge, buckwheat is placed in cold water and cooked for 20 minutes on low heat. When added to boiling water, the grains remain whole. If you add the buckwheat to flour, the dough is softer and needs less fat. As an easily digestible food, it is ideal for the diets of children, the elderly, the sick, and those engaging in hard physical labor. As a porridge, it can be eaten with milk, yogurt, and buttermilk or tomato juice with chopped onion, parsley or other herbs.

Preparing Grains

1. This is basic: grains need to be washed well in water several times. Millet, whole wheat, barley and rye can soak for a few hours before cooking, in the same water in which they will be cooked.

2. Preparation of grain is simple, but because they take longer to cook, it is good to prepare a larger quantity for several meals ahead. Cooked grain can be kept in the refrigerator for a few days and can be frozen. Frozen grains do not need to be cooked again. They can be added to hot meals or heated over steam.

3. Cooking in a pressure cooker: to one cup of whole grain (not rice) add two cups of water and cook for 1-1 ½ hours.

4. Cooking in a regular pot: to one cup of grain add three cups of water. Cook for approximately 2-3 hours. The pot must be covered, and stirring should be avoided as much as possible.

Crushed wheat, is cooked briefly for 5-10 minutes with minimum stirring to avoid pasting. Only fresh crushed wheat contains all of its vital elements. Like coffee, wheat can be ground in the coffee grinder just before use.

Ground grains (flour) are added to boiling water or milk to cook. To prevent clumping, flour can be first mixed with some cold water and then added to boiling water or milk.

Some grains can be combined and cooked together. Daily a minimum of 50g (16.75 ounces) of grain (3 tablespoons) is needed in any form (whole grains, flakes, porridge, pasta, sprouts, unglazed rice, etc.)

It is especially good to prepare breakfast from ground or crushed grains or grain flakes by allowing them to soak in sufficient water to cover them for 15-20 minutes. A spoonful of cream or yogurt can be added to taste along with:

– various seeds: flax, sesame, sunflower
– various ground nuts, walnuts, hazelnuts, almonds
– dried or grated fresh fruits
– honey as a sweetener

Instead of cream or yogurt, fruit juice can be used. A warm herbal drink is recommended after such a breakfast.

Grains in the diet represent the most important food of plant origin and should be used as much as possible in their raw state For them to be a healthy food neither chemical fertilizers nor chemicals should be used.

NUTS AND SEEDS are highly concentrated and caloric. They represent both food and medicine. They are rich in fat and need to be used prudently and sparingly. They contain large amounts of Vitamins E and F; lecithin which is indispensable for brain cells; sulfur, useful in the process of proper substance exchange and elimination of toxins from the liver; phosphorous for the nerves; and iron for the building of red blood cells.

Generally speaking the ability to use the biological components of this food is greater if it is eaten in its natural state. They must be chewed well so as to become an emulsion in the mouth. It is good to soak the nuts and seeds in a little water for 12-24 hours (this maximizes the effect of the enzymes), and then to crush them in a mixer or mortar and pestle. It is best to shell them immediately prior to usage. Nuts are susceptible to air and warmth and can turn rancid quickly. Their components can change. Fungus and toxins dangerous to health can affect them. It is thought that rancid food poses a cancer risk.

To make better use of iron from these sources, it is good to take them with an increased amount of Vitamin C or with rose hip tea that is high in Vitamin C. To the contrary, teas (such as black tea, sage, peppermint, ballmint or wormwood) contain tannin. Tannin blocks the use of iron.

WALNUT - *JUGLANS REGIA* – high in Vitamin B1, the essential fatty acids, and minerals, especially magnesium, zinc, sulfur, phosphorous, calcium, and iodine. Walnuts contribute to the strengthening of the immune system, build red blood cells and regulate blood pressure. They are recommended as medicinal in heart disease, urinary bladder stones and intestinal parasites. Young green walnuts, before they are ripened and formed, are rich in vitamin C and other vitamins. They serve as a medicine for anemia, especially in children.

HAZELNUT - *CORYLUS AVELLANA* - of all the nuts, it contains the most manganese which improves the exchange of substances in the system; it contains a high level of iron for the building of red blood cells; and is beneficial for the nerves. For a meal, 15-20 hazelnuts are sufficient because they contain a high quantity of fatty oil (60%) and 17% proteins.

ALMOND - *PRUNUS AMYGDALUS* - is rich in B Vitamins, especially B5 and B3. It is also rich in minerals, especially magnesium, calcium, iron, zinc and copper. Almonds are very good for strengthening a generally weak organism, for anemia, for the strengthening of the heart and the nervous system, against insomnia, for throat inflammations and for bronchitis. For respiratory problems, it is good to prepare a drink of ground almonds with warm milk, sweetened with honey. A well-chewed almond can facilitate the neutralization of increased levels of stomach acids.

CHESTNUT - *CASTANEA SATIVA* - is rich in only Vitamin B and phosphorus. Because of low sodium content, it is recommended for kidney disorders. Chestnuts are easily digestible and as a flour, rich in carbohydrates. They are useful in the diets of children and elderly. The flour is made by first removing the firm outside shell and then soaking the chestnut in warm water until the brown membrane can be easily removed. Chestnuts are then washed, dried and ground in a mixer. The flour can be used daily for soup, as a filling for cakes and can be mixed with other grains. 100g (33.5 ounces) of chestnuts has 215 kcal, and contains 3.4g (1.14 ounces) of proteins, 1.9g (0.64 ounces) of fats, and 46g (15.4 ounces) of carbohydrates.

SUNFLOWER SEEDS - *HELIANTHUS ANNUUS* – are rich in proteins, lecithin, enzymes, Vitamin E and minerals. Small seeds are used to produce oil and larger seeds are used for eating. Seeds can be eaten in their natural state. When ground they can be added to various fresh fruit salads, sweets, soups and stews. They can be combined with other seeds (sesame, flax) and added to cottage cheese. Adding sunflower seeds to bread gives bread a lovely flavor and retains freshness. Sunflower seeds are recommended for liver disease, spleen ailments, stomach ulcers, and rheumatism and as a protection against the effect of pollution, medication and radiation. 100g (33.5 ounces) of sunflower seeds contain 524 kcal, 27g (9.05 ounces) of proteins, 36g (12.06 ounces) of fats, and 23g (7.71 ounces) of carbohydrates.

SESAME SEEDS – *SESANUM* - contain quality fats, proteins, vitamins and minerals, especially iron and calcium. Because of large quantities of calcium, they are useful in fortifying soy milk, a nutritional substitute for children who cannot use animal and cow's milk. Due to their high iron content, they are also recommended for anemia. Roasted sesame seeds have a characteristically pleasant flavor and are used to flavor and decorate various foods, rolls, breads, and cakes. 100g (33.5 ounces) of sesame seeds contain 594 kcal, 20g (6.7 ounces) of proteins, 50g (16.75 ounces) of fat and 16g (5.36 ounces) of carbohydrates.

FLAXSEEDS - *LINUM USITATISSIMUM* - contain mucilage/gum, fatty oils, lecithin, proteins, and alpha-linoleic acids. It is a good remedy against gallstones. Oleaginous substances and flax oil have a calming effect. They prevent cramps and inflammation, soften the stool, aid in painless elimination from the intestines and the bladder, and aid in toxin elimination from the body. Flaxseed is beneficial for all skin inflammations and epidermal conditions. Alpha-linoleic acid in flaxseeds prevents the formation of blood clots, and a spoonful of flaxseeds a day protects against heart attacks. (University of Oslo, Professor of Biology A. Owren)

As a laxative, take one tablespoon of seeds in the morning and in the evening for chronic constipation. Its effect can be delayed (two-three days), and treatment needs to be continued regularly over a period of time. It can be used for weeks and even months (Kneipp) because it is completely harmless and has no side effects. Crushed flaxseeds mixed with honey clears the mucus in the lungs relieves coughs and soothes a raspy voice. A heated poultice of crushed seeds can be used for liver and gall ailments and for cramps caused by gallstones.

PUMPKINSEEDS - *CUCURBITA PEPO* - can be used in the diet as a substitute for walnuts, hazelnuts and almonds. They can be lightly roasted and ground. Washed and dried seeds are kept in a dry, cool place and shelled carefully prior to use. Care needs to be taken not to remove the light green coating under the outer shell, which contains valuable substances. Well-chewed seeds are excellent against intestinal parasites and tapeworm. Ground and mixed with the same amount of fresh warm milk without sugar, it is recommended for prostate problems. Because it contains essential fats and lecithin, it is also recommended for softening hardened arteries and because of salicylic acid, it acts to prevent blood clots.

PINE SEEDS - *PINUS SILVESTRIS* - are also edible. Other than containing more fat, in their composition, they do not differ from other seeds. 100g (33.5 ounces) of seeds contain 60g (201 ounces) of fat, 13g (4.23 ounces) of proteins, and 20.5g (6.73 ounces) of carbohydrates, and they have 674 kcal. The seeds can be eaten raw and added to other foods.

PEANUTS - *ARACHIS HYPOGAEA* - contain 40 - 50% of fatty oils and are rich in essential fatty acids, especially linoleic acid. They contain large amounts of Vitamin E, Vitamin B, starch, fiber, 20% protein, potassium, iron and calcium. Although, high in nutritional value, they need to be used moderately because 100g (33.5 ounces) contains 600 kcal. Seeds can be eaten roasted and can be served used as a substitute for coffee. Peanut oil is used for making margarine, in canning fish, in chocolate, cookies and baking.

Preparing Seeds

Sunflower, pumpkin, sesame, soy, and buckwheat seeds contain complete proteins of the highest value and are rich in minerals and vitamins.

Roasting seeds gives them a special flavor, especially when roasted on low temperature in a pan until they start to crackle. They can be eaten alone or as an additive to other dishes, for example, fresh cheese, yogurt, stewed fruits, vegetables, etc. They can also be ground.

Sprouting beans, grains and seeds increases their biological value by increasing the quality of their proteins and vitamins. Because of their nutritious and medicinal value, they are recommended in sickness and in health, especially as a preventative and a medicine against arteriosclerosis.

OTHER PROVISIONS OF PLANT ORIGIN

Vegetables, wild herbs and fruits are rich in water content and Vitamins A and C. The Vitamin C requirement is basically satisfied from the food group. Many of them, besides having antibiotic properties serve to neutralize nitrate and various other toxins. Because of this, they are ascribed as anti-carcinogenic.

Research has shown that a regular diet of this type of food has a great impact in treatment of many diseases of the digestive system, kidneys, nervous system and heart diseases. They also prevent arteriosclerosis, improve the blood and contribute to the maintenance of normal body weight and beauty. Because they contain a large quantity of water, minerals and fiber, many of them serve as a laxative to cleanse the organism.

VEGETABLES – have a great biological value only when they are grown in organically fertilized soil which is rich in valuable components and Oligocene elements.

Vegetables are best eaten picked fully ripe immediately after being harvested. It is then that they contain the most nutrition that the body use best.

Fresh vegetables abound in enzymes so the body can save its digestive juices. Such meals leave a pleasant sense of fullness and freshness because the system is less strained. It is good to eat fresh vegetables as often as possible in the form of different salads. Fresh vegetable juices, although healthy, cannot replace the whole plant because they contain only one component of it.

Depending on the part of the vegetable, which is eaten, vegetables can be classified as:

Green-leafed vegetables: spinach, Swiss chard, green salad, dandelion leaves, prickly lettuce, broccoli, sorrel, and endive. They are rich in iron, calcium, potassium, Vitamins C, B2, B9 and Provitamin A. The greener the vegetable the more Provitamin A it contains. Green cabbage has two-three times more iron and Vitamin C and 20 times more Provitamin A than white cabbage. It is the same with salads and other vegetables.

Bulb vegetables: garlic, red onions, scallions, leeks. They are rich in vitamins and minerals and contain antibacterial and antibiotic properties.

Fruit and Fruit vegetables: tomatoes, peppers, eggplants, cucumbers, pumpkins, gourds, cantaloupes and watermelons contain a high water content and are low in calories. They provide an excellent source of Vitamin C, B6, Provitamin A and potassium.

Root vegetables: carrots, celery, parsley, parsnips, beets, turnips, radishes and horseradish. They contain more carbohydrates and less water, thus providing a good source of energy. They are rich in vitamins, minerals and elements in traces significant for health.

Tuberous vegetables: potatoes. Because of their nutritional value and starch content, they are often set apart from other vegetables. They are a good supplement and substitute for bread and pasta since they contain less calories and many minerals such as potassium, calcium, magnesium, iron, and Vitamins C and B.

Legumes: lentils, soy beans, beans, peas, chick peas, chick beans are vegetables, but have their own classification because of their greater content of quality proteins. They are rich in vitamins and minerals, especially Vitamin C and iron.

SPINACH - *SPINACEA OLERACEA* - **100g (33.5 ounces) = 18 kcal – total of minerals, 1400 mg**. Has a very low energy value because it contains small quantities of protein, carbohydrates and fats. It contains various minerals and is especially high in potassium (465 mg) and iron (3.5g or 1.15 ounces). Because of its high iron content, it is especially recommended for anemia. Recent studies have confirmed that the body uses this form of iron very slowly and poorly. Spinach is rich in Vitamin A (8190 lJ), Vitamin C (10 mg) and the Vitamin B complex (B1, B2, B3, B5, and B6) and it is especially rich in folic acid (B9). It also contains fiber important for digestion and for cleansing the organism from toxic waste. Spinach is called the 'king of green leaf vegetables.' Its significance in the diet of children, adults, the elderly and the ill, is great. [32]

[32] Cf. SPRČIĆ, Josip, *Unpublished document*, Metković, 1996., p.p. 7-13, 64-74 i 132-135. (pp. 181-220 translated by Jamie Marich, corrected by Rita Falsetto)

XIV. ANOTHER SIDE OF FASTING

14.1. HEALTHY, BEAUTIFUL, RICH

From literature, it is possible to say that the world has discovered fasting, but too late. Late simply because fasting was discovered when man had already become sick, lost his beautiful figure and paid much for this. Not a single pound is gained accidentally. It has to be earned daily by hard work. A great deal has to be eaten if a person is to gain even a single pound. He has to eat breakfast, lunch and dinner regularly and has to snack between meals. So, in order that a person gain many pounds, he has to eat a great deal. In order to eat a great deal, he has to prepare a great deal. In order to prepare a great deal, he has to buy a great deal. In order to be able to buy a great deal he has to have money. In order to have money, he has to work to earn it. In the end, he gains weight, loses his beautiful figure and gets sick more easily.

When he gets sick, he has to find a clinic and clinical therapy is very expensive. So it happens that it costs the person a great deal to gain weight, and therapy is not cheap. In this way, a person becomes sick and poor.

This concentric circle can easily be avoided if we accept Our Lady's programme. Whoever fasts for two days a week, can more easily retain his ideal weight, pays less for food, stays healthy more easily and will not have to pay for therapy. In this way, a person who accepts Our Lady's programme remains healthy, beautiful and rich. Whoever takes his life seriously will accept Our Lady's programme!

14.2. A NASTY PERSON

A pilgrim who accepted Our Lady's program of fasting once said to me, "I fast for two days a week as Our Lady asks but on fast days, I am a very nasty person."

I congratulated him.

He then said to me, "Father, did you understand what I just said to you? When I fast I am a nasty person."

I told him that I understood what he said and repeated, "Congratulations!"

He looked at me surprised and again asked, "Why are you congratulating me?"

I responded, "I congratulate you! You are a nasty person for only two days a week. Those who don't fast are nasty all seven days, they just don't see it!"

14.3. FASTING AND BEING NERVOUS

A pilgrim asked me, "Which is better -- to eat and be pleasant or to fast and be aggressive and aggitated?"

I responded, "It is best to fast and be pleasant and serene."

Then I added, "If only those who fasted were aggitated, there wouldn't be many aggitated and unpleasant people in the world! So why are others nervous and unpleasant? How many times have we eaten, drunk and had everything, but were still nervous and reacted with aggitation? Fasting does not create anything new. First of all, it shows us what we are like and when we come to understand that, we can then begin anew."

14.4. EXPERIENCE OF CARMELO PUZZOLO

Carmelo Puzzolo is the artist who made the bronze reliefs of the Way of the Cross on Cross Mountain and of the Mysteries of the Rosary on the Hill of Apparitions in Medjugorje. He gives witness to what it was like when he started to fast.

His first thought on a Wednesday and a Friday was always, "Today there is no breakfast!" Consequently, his first feeling was one of hunger, even though he would eat more on Tuesday and Thursday evenings to get him through the fast days more easily.

When on fast days he worked on Church frescos or elsewhere, he would smell every aroma from every kitchen in the surrounding area. Interestingly, on Thursday and Saturday mornings, he didn't think or feel the same way; even though, physically speaking, it would have been more natural for him to feel hunger on those days.

This experience shows us that when it comes to fasting, we behave like addicts. When we start to fast, until we receive inner freedom, problems are created only by our own addiction.

14.5. CATHEDRAL OR A SMALL CHAPEL – ONE EVIDENCE AGAINST FASTING

In front of the Church in Medjugorje, I met a priest who was over six feet tall and only a little less wide. I walked up to him, patted him on the shoulder and jokingly said to him, "Father it would be good to respect Our Lady's program!"

He looked down at me and in a deep voice said, "Pardon me, what programme?"

I explained to him that Our Lady is asking for two days of fasting a week, on Wednesdays and Fridays and told him that this wouldn't be bad for him either.

A broad pleasant smile came across his face and jokingly he said, "Absolutely not that!"

Surprised I asked him, "Why not? Coming to Medjugorje, you entered into the school of Our Lady?"

He smiled even more good-naturedly and said, "That I do not accept! When the the Lord gave me a cathedral, I am not to make a small chapel of it!"

We both laughed heartily and I added, "Then protect the cathedral and patiently keep it intact so that it can remain mobile!"

I promised him that I would share this story with every group because it is the only proof against fasting. In further conversion I found out that he was a basketball player and that, after an active involvment in sports, he felt a calling to the priesthood. He finished Theology and became a priest. The comfortable priestly life made him nearly as wide as he is tall, but he patiently carries his 'cathedral'. The message is simple: all of you who have painstakingly built your cathedrals, protect them! Just know that they will be cleaner if you also fasted!

CARDINAL JOSEPH RATZINGER ON FASTING

A well-known Italian author, Vittorio Messori, spoke with Cardinal Joseph Ratzinger, Prefect of the Congregation for the Doctrine of the Faith, and published this interview in book form. Some of the questions and answers pertaining to fasting are paraphrased here.

Vittorio Messori: Apparitions can be either true or untrue, and 'messages from Marian apparitions' are problematic particuarly because they evidently contradict some 'post- Council positions' . . .

Cardinal Ratzinger interrupted the question and said, "I want to accentuate that I do not like the expressions: 'pre' or 'post' council. If we were to accept this, it would mean that we accept a form of a break in the history of the Church. In the 'apparitions', the corporeal is emphasized (the sign of the Cross, blessed water, a call to fasting), but all of that is completely in accord with the Second Vatican Council; because the oneness of man is emphasized and, by that, the incarnation of the Spirit in the body."

VM: Fasting you just mentioned has a central place in many apparitions?

Cardinal Ratzinger: "To fast means to accept the essential viewpoint of a Christian life. It is also necessary to discover the corporeal aspect of faith: refraining from food is such an aspect. Sexuality and nutrition belong to the fundamental elements of human corporality: a decreasing understanding of chastity is taking place simultaneously with a decreased understanding of fasting. All of this comes from the same root: the current darkening of the eschatological tension. This means that the expectation of the eternal life, which is essential for Christian faith, is disappearing. Chastity and occasional renunciation of food witness that eternal life, which is already among us, awaits us

because 'the world in its present form is passing away.' "
(1 Cor 7,31)

"Without chastity and without fasting the Church is no longer the Church because it becomes analogous to the world. That is why we need to take our brothers from the eastern churches as an example: those who are still today the great teachers of true Christian asceticism."

VM: Your Emminence, if the 'physical expressions' of faith are disappearing among us Catholics (while they are perhaps alive in some elite groups) then the attitude of the institutional Church was also a cause of this: after the Council, directives came from Rome moderating the fasting on Fridays, night vigils, times of fasting, Advent and other 'special times'?

Cardinal Ratzinger: "This stands, but the intention was good. It was to avoid the doubt of legalism and the temptation of having the faith reduced to external practices. One thing is clear: fasting, renunciation and other 'penitential practices' must continue to remain a personal responsibility of the individual. It is also important for us to return to the communal forms of ecclesiastical penance. Additionally, particularily in this world in which many people are dying of hunger, we must show with love, the visible communal witness of freely willed renunciation of food." [33]

[33] Ratzinger, Cardinal Joseph, *Zur Lage des Glaubens, ein Gesprächt mit Vittorio Messori,* München, 1984., pp. 115-116.

BIBLIOGRAPHY

AURELIUS AUGUSTINUS, *Der Nutzen des Fastens*, Augustinus, Verlag, Würzburg, 1958.

BUCHINGER, Otto, dr. med. i BUCHINGER, Andreas, *Das heilende Fasten,* Dr. Werner Jopp Verlag, 4th printing, Wiesbaden, 1991.

BUCHINGER, Otto jun., *Das Heilfasten und seine Hilfsmethoden als biologischer Weg*, Hypokrates Verlag, 22nd printing, Stuttgart, 1992.

Catechism of the Catholic Church, Veritas-Libreria Editrice Vaticana, Dublin, 1994.

FAHRNER, Heinz, *Fasten als Therapie, Physiologie und Pathophysiologie, Methodik, Indikationen und Verläufe, Psychologische Aspekte*, Hypokrates Verlag, Stuttgart, 1991.

FISTLER, Mary, *"And then they will fast in that day"*, Thesis, Pontifical University, St. Thomas Academy, Rome, 1998.

FRIEBEL, Gisela, *Gesundheit fast zum Nulltarif,* Vier Flamingos Verlag, Rheine, 1991.

Gospel of Life, Pope John Paul II, Rome, at St. Peter's, March 25, 1995.

GRUYTER, Walter de, *Theologische Realenzyklopödie*, Edition XI, Berlin - New York, 1983., und *Reallexikon für Antike und Christentum*, 7th Edition, Stuttgart, 1969.

GRÜN, Anselm, OSB, *Fasten*, Vier–Türme-Verlag, Münsterschwarzach, 1984.

HERCEG, Father Mladen, *Jeka Tišine*, Zagreb, for private use. 1998.

LEJEUNE, René, *Jeüne, guérison and fęte du corps et de l'esprit*, Parvis, 3rd Issue, Hauteville, 1991.

LÉON-DUFOUR, Xavier, *Dictionary of Biblical Theology*, 4th Printing, Zagreb, 1993.

MILLER, B. *Die Weisung der Väter*, Freiburg, 1965.

NIESSEN, Franz, *Der Dinge bestes: Brot*, Verlag Butzon & Bercker, Kevelaer, 1983.

PAENITEMINI *(Apostolic Constitution On Penance)*, Pope Paul VI, Issued on February 17, 1966.

RATZINGER, Cardinal Joseph, *Zur Lage des Glaubens, ein Gesprächt mit Vittorio Messori*, München, 1984.

RECKINGER, Fançois, *Gott begegnen in der Zeit: unser Kirchenjahr*, Verlag bonifatius Drickerei, Paderborn, 1986.

Roman Missal, Catholic Book Publishing Co., New York, 1985.

ROMANO, Bruno, *Il digiuno, come salvarsi la vita*, Edizioni mediterranee, Roma, 1991.

SCHMEMANN, Alexander, *Die große Fastenzeit, Askese und Liturgie in der Orthodoxen Kirche*, Band 2, aus dem Englischem von Elmar Kalthoff.

SCHMEMANN, Alexander, *Jeûne et liturgie,* IRENIKON, Tome XXVII, Prieuré Bénédictin D'Amay, Chevetogne, Belgija, 1954.

SEEGER, Hans-Karl, *Heilfasten – das Leben neu bedenken*, Butzon & Bercker, Kevelaer, 1998.

SPRČIĆ, Josip, *Unpublished document*, Metković, 1996.

VOGÜE, Adalbert de, *To Love Fasting, The Monastic Experience*, Petersham, MA 01366, 1994.

Made in the USA
Charleston, SC
13 July 2012